BAPTISTWAY ADULT BIBLE STUDY GUIDE®
LARGE PRINT EDITION

The Gospel of Luke
JESUS' PERSONAL TOUCH

BOB DEFOOR
PAM GIBBS
JESSE RINCONES
JULIE WOOD

BAPTISTWAYPRESS®
Dallas, Texas

*The Gospel of Luke: Jesus' Personal Touch—BaptistWay
Adult Bible Study Guide®—Large Print Edition*

Copyright © 2013 by BAPTISTWAY PRESS®.
All rights reserved.
Printed in the United States of America.

No part of this book may be used or reproduced in any manner whatsoever without written permission except in the case of brief quotations. For information, contact BAPTISTWAY PRESS, Baptist General Convention of Texas, 333 North Washington, Dallas, TX 75246–1798.

BAPTISTWAY PRESS® is registered in U.S. Patent and Trademark Office.

Unless otherwise indicated, all Scripture quotations in lessons 1–13 are taken from the HOLY BIBLE, NEW INTERNATIONAL VERSION®. Copyright © 1973, 1978, 1984 Biblica. Used by permission of Zondervan. All rights reserved. NIV84 refers to this edition of the New International Version.

All Scripture quotations marked NASB are taken from the 1995 update of the New American Standard Bible®, Copyright © The Lockman Foundation 1960, 1962, 1963, 1968, 1971, 1972, 1973, 1975, 1977, 1995. Used by permission. NASB refers to this edition of the New American Standard Bible®.

All Scripture quotations marked NRSV are taken from the New Revised Standard Version Bible, copyright 1989, Division of Christian Education of the National Council of the Churches of Christ in the United States of America. Used by permission. All rights reserved.

BAPTISTWAY PRESS® Leadership Team
Executive Director, Baptist General Convention of Texas: David Hardage
Director, Church Ministry Resources: Chris Liebrum
Director, Bible Study/Discipleship Team: Phil Miller
Publisher, BaptistWay Press®: Scott Stevens

Cover and Interior Design and Production: Desktop Miracles, Inc.
Printing: Data Reproductions Corporation

First edition: December 2013
ISBN–13: 978-1-938355-10-3

How to Make the Best Use of This Issue

Whether you're the teacher or a student—

1. Start early in the week before your class meets.

2. Overview the study. Review the table of contents and read the study introduction. Try to see how each lesson relates to the overall study.

3. Use your Bible to read and consider prayerfully the Scripture passages for the lesson. (You'll see that each writer has chosen a favorite translation for the lessons in this issue. You're free to use the Bible translation you prefer and compare it with the translation chosen for that unit, of course.)

4. After reading all the Scripture passages in your Bible, then read the writer's comments. The comments are intended to be an aid to your study of the Bible.

5. Read the small articles—"sidebars"—in each lesson. They are intended to provide additional, enrichment information and inspiration and to encourage thought and application.

6. Try to answer for yourself the questions included in each lesson. They're intended to encourage further

thought and application, and they can also be used in the class session itself.

If you're the teacher—

A. Do all of the things just mentioned, of course. As you begin the study with your class, be sure to find a way to help your class know the date on which each lesson will be studied. You might do this in one or more of the following ways:

- In the first session of the study, briefly overview the study by identifying for your class the date on which each lesson will be studied. Lead your class to write the date in the table of contents on page 11 and on the first page of each lesson.

- Make and post a chart that indicates the date on which each lesson will be studied.

- If all of your class has e-mail, send them an e-mail with the dates the lessons will be studied.

- Provide a bookmark with the lesson dates. You may want to include information about your church and then use the bookmark as an outreach tool, too. A model for a bookmark can be downloaded from www.baptistwaypress.org on the Adults—Bible Studies page.

- Develop a sticker with the lesson dates, and place it on the table of contents or on the back cover.

B. Get a copy of the *Teaching Guide*, a companion piece to this *Study Guide*. The *Teaching Guide* contains additional Bible comments plus two teaching plans. The teaching plans in the *Teaching Guide* are intended to provide practical, easy-to-use teaching suggestions that will work in your class.

C. After you've studied the Bible passage, the lesson comments, and other material, use the teaching suggestions in the *Teaching Guide* to help you develop your plan for leading your class in studying each lesson.

D. Teaching resource items for use as handouts are available free at www.baptistwaypress.org.

E. Additional Bible study comments on the lessons are available online. Call 1–866–249–1799 or e-mail baptistway@texasbaptists.org to order *Adult Online Bible Commentary*. It is available only in electronic format (PDF) from our website, www.baptistwaypress.org. The price of these comments for the entire study is $6 for individuals and $25 for a group of five. A church or class that participates in our advance order program for free shipping can receive *Adult Online Bible Commentary* free. Call 1–866–249–1799 or see www.baptistwaypress.org to purchase or for information on participating in our free shipping program for the next study.

F. Additional teaching plans are also available in electronic format (PDF) by calling 1–866–249–1799. The price of these additional teaching plans for the entire study is $5 for an individual and $20 for a group of five. A church or class that participates in our advance order program for free shipping can receive *Adult Online Teaching Plans* free. Call 1–866–249–1799 or see www.baptistwaypress.org for information on participating in our free shipping program for the next study.

G. You also may want to get the enrichment teaching help that is provided on the Internet by the *Baptist Standard* at www.baptiststandard.com. (Other class participants may find this information helpful, too.) The *Baptist Standard* is available online for an annual subscription rate of $10. Subscribe online at www.baptiststandard.com or call 214–630–4571. (A free ninety-day trial subscription is currently available.)

H. Enjoy leading your class in discovering the meaning of the Scripture passages and in applying these passages to their lives.

Do you use a Kindle?

This BaptistWay *Adult Bible Study Guide* plus *Hebrews and the Letters of Peter; Guidance for the Seasons of Life; Living Generously for Jesus' Sake; Profiles in Character; Psalms: Songs from the Heart of Faith; Amos, Hosea, Isaiah, Micah; The Gospel of Matthew; The Gospel of Mark; The Gospel of John: Part One; The Gospel of John: Part Two; The Book of Acts: Time to Act on Acts 1:8;* and *The Corinthian Letters: Imperatives for an Imperfect Church* are now available in a Kindle edition. The easiest way to find these materials is to search for "BaptistWay" on your Kindle or go to www.amazon.com/kindle and do a search for "BaptistWay." The Kindle edition can be studied not only on a Kindle but also on a PC, Mac, iPhone, iPad, Blackberry, or Android phone using the Kindle app available free from amazon.com/kindle.

AUDIO BIBLE STUDY LESSONS

Do you want to use your walk/run/ride, etc. time to study the Bible? Or maybe you're looking for a way to study the Bible when you just can't find time to read? Or maybe you know someone who has difficulty seeing to read even our *Large Print Study Guide*?

Then try our audio Bible study lessons, available on *Living Generously for Jesus' Sake*; *Profiles in Character*; *Amos, Hosea, Isaiah, Micah*; *The Gospel of Matthew*; *The Gospel of Mark*; *The Gospel of Luke*; *The Gospel of John: Part One*; *The Gospel of John: Part Two*; *The Book of Acts*; *The Corinthian Letters*; *Galatians and 1 & 2 Thessalonians*; and *The Letters of James and John*. For more information or to order, call 1–866–249–1799 or e-mail baptistway@ texasbaptists.org. The files are downloaded from our website. You'll need an audio player or phone that plays MP3 files (like an iPod®, but many MP3 players are available), or you can listen on a computer.

Writers for This Study Guide

Bob DeFoor of Harrodsburg, Kentucky, wrote **lessons one through three.** Dr. DeFoor served more than forty years as pastor of churches in Kentucky and Georgia, serving the last twenty-eight prior to retirement as pastor of Harrodsburg Baptist Church. Both Bob and his wife Sandy are native Georgians, and both are graduates of Baylor University, Waco, Texas.

Jesse Rincones wrote **lessons four and five and the Christmas lesson.** Jesse has served for 10 years as pastor of Alliance Church in Lubbock, Texas. He graduated from Texas Tech University with a B.A. in Mathematics and earned a Juris Doctor degree from the Texas Tech School of Law. Jesse currently serves as Executive Director of the Hispanic Baptist Convention of Texas and has served on the boards of Hereford Regional Medical Center, Pray Lubbock, Mission Lubbock and Baptist University of the Americas. He is married to Brenda and they share four great kids.

Pam Gibbs wrote **lessons six through nine** in this *Adult Bible Study Guide* as well as "Teaching Plans" for these lessons in the *Adult Bible Teaching Guide*. Pam is a freelance writer and speaker who lives in Nashville, TN, where she serves as the youth minister at Bellevue Baptist Church. A native Texan, Pam is a graduate of Southwestern Baptist Theological Seminary and has been involved in ministry for over 20 years. She loves spending time with her husband Jim and daughter Kaitlyn.

Julie (Brown) Wood wrote **lessons ten through thirteen.** She is a graduate of Hardin-Simmons University and Southwestern Baptist Theological Seminary. She loves ministering with her husband, Dr. Darin Wood, pastor of Central Baptist Church in Jacksonville, Texas, and being mother to their son, Joshua. A former children's minister and worship leader, she now serves as a freelance writer and pianist for Jacksonville Independent School District choirs.

The Gospel of Luke: Jesus' Personal Touch

UNIT THREE
Answering Personal Questions

Introducing

THE GOSPEL OF LUKE:
Jesus' Personal Touch

Approaching This Study of the Gospel of Luke

In order to touch someone we have to move in close. Sometimes that can require crossing barriers of distance and inconvenience as well as the willingness to move past racial, social, economic and religious stereotypes. Personal sacrifice and service can also bring healing and hope to those who are in desperate need. The Gospel of Luke reveals Jesus as the Promised Messiah who brings his personal touch to a world in need.

Throughout the Gospel of Luke there are accounts of Jesus becoming personally involved in the lives of others. We see him meeting personal needs—often in miraculous ways, we find him challenging people to make significant personal choices, and we also have the opportunity to listen to him answer some difficult personal questions.

As we move through this study of the Gospel of Luke, the stories and people we encounter will confront us with personal questions about our attitudes and actions as followers of Christ. We will have the chance to consider the cost of discipleship and will be encouraged to face the future with faith rather than fear.

We can rejoice that Jesus came to earth, bringing his personal touch to meet our greatest need. He is indeed good news of great joy for all people!

Since the beginning of our BaptistWay Bible study series, we have focused on the Gospel of Luke three times previously. (This particular study appears in our thirteenth year of publishing ongoing curriculum.) The first study was titled *The Gospel of Luke: Meeting Jesus Again. Anew.* This happened to be the first ongoing study produced by BaptistWay. The second study was titled *The Gospel of Luke: Parables Jesus Told* and the third was *The Gospel of Luke: Good News of Great Joy.* Each of these studies—this one as well as the previous three—is different from the others in its approach to the individual lessons.[1]

We think studying Scriptures directly about Jesus on a regular basis is important, so we provide a study of a Gospel each year. Each study begins with a new emphasis, and fresh outlines and lessons are created.

A Little Background on the Gospel of Luke

The Gospel of Luke, probably written around A.D. 60–61, is a carefully researched account of the life of Jesus Christ. Luke, a Gentile physician and a traveling companion of the Apostle Paul, used great care and precision in writing this Gospel so his readers would be convinced of the truth of who Jesus is: the Promised Messiah and Savior of the world. He also emphasizes the personal touch of Jesus that brings healing and salvation to everyone, regardless of their social status or cultural and religious background.

The Gospel of Luke and the Book of Acts (also written by Luke) when combined, account for the largest number of verses written by a New Testament author. Luke was also a historian and his inclusion of significant dates and people enhance the veracity of his claims about the life of Christ. Luke was an evangelist who employed the accounts of eyewitnesses as well as corroboration from ancient prophecy to confirm his message to his friend Theophilus, and to us.

Jesus' Personal Touch in Our Day

How should Jesus' personal touch affect and influence his followers today? How can we imitate his attitude and actions? The Gospel of Luke continually points to the priority of a relationship with Jesus that proves itself in faithful living. Luke also reminds his readers that God knows and cares about all of their personal needs and is more than willing and able to meet them.

We have all been shaped by the personal touch of others. Let these stories from the Gospel of Luke remind you of Jesus' touch on your life and inspire you to follow him with increased faith. Let Jesus' words encourage you to be an extension of his personal touch in the world today.

How the Study Is Developed

Unit one, "Meeting Personal Needs" contains five lessons from Luke 5–13. These lessons reveal Jesus' willingness to overcome barriers to meet various needs. Lessons one and two explore Jesus' ability to provide physical and spiritual healing, as well as his power over death. In lessons three and four, Jesus uses parables to destroy accepted boundaries of love and service. He also challenges attitudes toward material wealth and the confidence to trust in God's provision. In lesson five, Jesus provides healing for a woman and uses the occasion to point to the surpassing value of people over man-made religious rules.

Unit two, "Making a Personal Choice" is comprised of four lessons from Luke 14–19 that present challenging questions for those who choose to follow Christ. Lesson six focuses on the cost of discipleship while lesson seven warns about the danger of spiritual pride. Lesson eight confronts disciples in the area of their priorities and lesson nine calls us to evaluate our response to the personal invitation of Jesus. The lessons are helpful reminders of how choices produce character.

Unit three, "Answering Personal Questions" traces Jesus' responses to various questions from Luke 20–24. His answers speak to his authority (lesson ten), the future (lesson 11), and his identity (lesson twelve.) In lesson thirteen, Jesus uses his encounter on the road to Emmaus to confirm his resurrection and explain the Scriptures to two despondent disciples.

Note: Since the time of the first release of these materials includes the Christmas holiday, a Christmas lesson is included to meet the needs of churches who wish to have an emphasis on Christmas at this time.

UNIT ONE: MEETING PERSONAL NEEDS

Lesson 1	Physical and Spiritual Healing	Luke 5:12–26
Lesson 2	A Humble Request and a Hopeless Situation	Luke 7:1–17
Lesson 3	Love Without Limits	Luke 10:25–37
Lesson 4	Greed vs. Need	Luke 12:13–34
Lesson 5	Focused on People, Not Rules	Luke 13:10–17

UNIT TWO: MAKING A PERSONAL CHOICE

Lesson 6	Sacrifice or Security?	Luke 14:25–35

UNIT THREE: ANSWERING PERSONAL QUESTIONS

Additional Resources for Studying the *Gospel of Luke*[2]

William Barclay. *The Gospel of Luke.* Revised edition. Louisville, Kentucky: Westminster John Knox Press, 1975.

Kenneth L. Barker and John R. Kohlenberger III. *The Expositor's Bible Commentary—Abridged Edition: New Testament.* Grand Rapids, Michigan: Zondervan, 1994.

Bruce Barton, Philip Comfort, Grant Osborne, Linda K. Taylor, and Dave Veerman. *Life Application New Testament Commentary.* Carol Stream, Illinois: Tyndale House Publishers, Inc., 2001.

Darrell L. Bock. *Luke.* The NIV Application Commentary. Grand Rapids, Michigan: Zondervan, 1996.

Craig S. Keener. *IVP Bible Background Commentary: New Testament.* Downers Grove, Illinois: InterVarsity Press, 1993.

Leon Morris. *Tyndale New Testament Commentaries, Volume 3: Luke.* Downers Grove, Illinois: InterVarsity Press, 1988.

John Nolland. Luke. Volume 35 of *Word Biblical Commentary.* Nashville: Nelson Reference & Electronic, 1989.

A.T. Robertson. *Word Pictures in the New Testament: Concise Edition.* Nashville, Tennessee: Holman Bible Publishers, 2000.

Robert H. Stein. *Luke.* The New American Commentary. Volume 24. Nashville, Tennessee: B&H Publishing Group, 1992.

Ray Summers. *Commentary on Luke.* Waco, Texas: Word Books, 1972.

Spiros Zodhiates and Warren Baker. *Hebrew-Greek Key Word Study Bible, New International Version.* Grand Rapids, Michigan: Zondervan, 1996.

N O T E S

1. See www.baptistwaypress.org.

2. Listing a book does not imply full agreement by the writers or BAPTISTWAY PRESS® with all of its comments.

Meeting Personal Needs

Unit one, "Meeting Personal Needs" contains five lessons from Luke 5–13. Lessons one and two explore Jesus' ability to provide physical and spiritual healing, as well as his power over death. In lessons three and four, Jesus uses parables to destroy accepted boundaries of love and service and to challenge attitudes toward material wealth and our trust of God's provision. In lesson five, Jesus provides healing for a woman and uses the occasion to point to the surpassing value of people over man-made religious rules.

UNIT ONE: MEETING PERSONAL NEEDS

FOCAL TEXT
Luke 5:12–26

BACKGROUND
Luke 4:38–44; 5:12–6:11

LESSON ONE

Physical and Spiritual Healing

MAIN IDEA

Jesus' healing touch met the physical and spiritual needs of a leper and a paralytic.

QUESTION TO EXPLORE

In what ways do we need to experience Jesus' healing touch?

STUDY AIM

To describe Jesus' encounters with a leper and a paralytic and to identify areas where I may need his healing touch

QUICK READ

Though the form of healing may not be the same as with the leper or paralytic, God helps us to deal positively with whatever affects us negatively. God still heals, restores, and redirects us.

Preaching, teaching, and healing are often identified as the three-fold ministry of Jesus. Jesus came telling the good news of the gospel, teaching his disciples through the ages about God and the godly life, and bringing wholeness and health to many people. This study of the Book of Luke focuses on his personal touch in meeting the needs of all people. For more information on this study, see the article, "Introducing *The Gospel of Luke: Jesus' Personal Touch*" in this *Study Guide*.[1]

Today's Scripture deals with two persons whom Jesus healed. One was cast out from his society, a diseased man who people avoided. The second was of such great concern to his friends that they literally went *through the roof* in order to get Jesus to help them. These two encounters encourage us to turn to Jesus for help in dealing with our own needs for healing. These needs could include healing of the body, emotions, self-perception, or relationships. Jesus cares about our needs and is willing to extend his healing touch.

LUKE 5:12–26

12 While Jesus was in one of the towns, a man came along who was covered with leprosy. When he saw Jesus, he fell with his face to the ground and begged him, "Lord, if you are willing, you can make me clean." 13 Jesus reached out his hand and touched the man. "I

am willing," he said. "Be clean!" And immediately the leprosy left him. [14] Then Jesus ordered him, "Don't tell anyone, but go, show yourself to the priest and offer the sacrifices that Moses commanded for your cleansing, as a testimony to them." [15] Yet the news about him spread all the more, so that crowds of people came to hear him and to be healed of their sicknesses. [16] But Jesus often withdrew to lonely places and prayed. [17] One day as he was teaching, Pharisees and teachers of the law, who had come from every village of Galilee and from Judea and Jerusalem, were sitting there. And the power of the Lord was present for him to heal the sick. [18] Some men came carrying a paralytic on a mat and tried to take him into the house to lay him before Jesus. [19] When they could not find a way to do this because of the crowd, they went up on the roof and lowered him on his mat through the tiles into the middle of the crowd, right in front of Jesus. [20] When Jesus saw their faith, he said, "Friend, your sins are forgiven." [21] The Pharisees and the teachers of the law began thinking to themselves, "Who is this fellow who speaks blasphemy? Who can forgive sins but God alone?" [22] Jesus knew what they were thinking and asked, "Why are you thinking these things in your hearts? [23] Which is easier: to say, 'Your sins are forgiven,' or to say, 'Get up and walk'? [24] But that you may know that the Son of Man has authority on earth to forgive sins . . . ." He said to the paralyzed man, "I tell you, get up, take your mat and go home." [25] Immediately he stood up in front of them, took what he had been lying on and went home praising God. ²⁶ Everyone was amazed and gave praise to God. They were filled with awe and said, "We have seen remarkable things today."

God's Love for Outcasts (5:12–16)

Leprosy was a dreaded disease during biblical times and is still common in many parts of the world. It manifests itself in a variety of types, but commonly a person with leprosy has skin lesions and nodules. The nerves can become so affected that one loses the sensation of touch or even pain. Left untreated, leprosy can lead to numbness in the legs and arms, disfigurement, and can be the cause of many accidents. Though we know much about leprosy today and can successfully treat it, people knew little about it centuries ago. People in biblical times practiced the best preventive medicine they knew—to avoid leprosy they avoided close contact with those who were infected. In those days leprosy was as devastating as AIDS or cancer is in our time. The additional implications of the disease related to social interaction and religious involvement increased the lepers' misery.

Leviticus 13 and 14 provided instruction for how people were to deal with leprosy. A key part of the prevention of leprosy involved lepers having to continually identify themselves as *unclean.* Other health problems carried a similar penalty, but lepers were a particular object of scorn. Not only did they suffer with an awful disease, there was also a commonly held misunderstanding about lepers. Many religious people believed that lepers were receiving a deserved penalty, in that their physical condition was caused by their sinfulness. By Jesus' time, people generally avoided lepers and lepers generally avoided other people. Most people were fearful of coming into contact with a leper.

In light of the first century world, Jesus' actions with the leper were even more amazing. Jesus did not tell him to stay away or rebuke him. Jesus did not avoid him or run from him. The man fell at Jesus' feet, face down, and begged Jesus to "make me clean" (Luke 5:12). The man wondered if Jesus was willing to heal him. Then Jesus touched him, saying "I am willing" (5:13). In touching him, Jesus violated the religious rules regarding leprosy; however, his touch did not heal the leper. But when Jesus said, "Be clean," (5:13) the man was immediately healed.

Jesus healed in many ways. He healed a royal official's son in Cana by long distance. Jesus did so because the man believed Jesus could heal his son, and then asked him to do so (John 4:43–54). He healed a woman with an issue of blood after she touched the hem of his garment. The healing did not happen, however, because of her touch, but because of her faith to touch and believe in Jesus (Mark 5:25–34). He spit on some dirt and made mud, then placed the dirt on the eyes of a man who was born blind. Jesus then told the man to wash in the pool of Siloam. The blind man obeyed Jesus and he "went and washed, and came home seeing" (John 9:7).

Jesus healed people. He had the compassion, power, and authority to do so. The crowds liked what Jesus did, though the first century Jewish leaders were confounded by his actions. They should have rejoiced at what happened to so many people; instead they felt threatened by Jesus and his growing popularity. Jesus knew that some of his popularity was due to his miracles (see John 2:22–25), not just those that brought healing, but also those that revealed his power to calm the sea and feed thousands with a limited supply of fish and bread.

Jesus could have spent all his time in individual healing experiences or he could have announced, "Everyone, be healed!" and that would have taken care of leprosy and all diseases. As nice as that would have been, the day of no more mourning or sorrow, no more sickness or pain (Rev. 21:1–4) is still in the future. Jesus did not heal everyone because that was not his purpose. In the process of his ministry, however, he helps us understand that all sin brings suffering, but our sin is not necessarily the reason for all our sufferings. Suffering is part of our common humanity.

When Jesus stopped to heal the leper, it was not the time for a seminar on leprosy; it was a time to exercise his compassion and prerogative as the Son of God to heal one person. Jesus instructed the man to show himself to the priest, which followed the Old Testament ritual

(Lev. 14:2–32). He also told the man not to tell anyone what happened, but word spread quickly, so much so that "crowds of people came to hear him and to be healed" (5:15). Apparently the man was so blessed he could not restrain his tongue.

Prayer, God's Way to Renewal (5:16)

"But Jesus often withdrew to lonely places and prayed" (5:16). Today's Scripture is about two people who were healed: a leper and a paralytic. The linking verse between the two stories does not indicate that these events followed quickly in time. Underline the word *often* in this verse. After Jesus healed the leper, he turned aside to spend time alone with his Heavenly Father. We certainly can learn from that. Rather than building on his popularity as a miracle worker, Jesus paused to pray and spend time alone with God. Could that be a key to his power and perspective on life? How could our lives be affected if we adjusted our calendars and rearranged our priorities to spend time alone with God?

Spiritual and Physical Healing (5:17–26)

Imagine the scene. The master teacher and preacher had the right audience. The big time religious leaders were present and the house was packed. We do not have a record of what Jesus was teaching, though every moment with Jesus would have been a teachable moment. The teaching time soon became a healing time. Doorways were blocked ⸱ by the committed and curious people, and by those who were sick and wanted to be healed. Into that scene, four latecomers arrived, carrying a man on a stretcher. They could not get in. They all believed Jesus could heal the sick man, but they could not get to Jesus. They were not deterred. They took the man to the roof, made an opening in the roof, and lowered the man into Jesus' presence. What a scene that must have been. Can you imagine the impact on the crowd?

It was a good show, but Jesus saw something else. Jesus saw their faith. That statement could refer to the faith of the four friends, but it probably refers to the faith of five people (the paralytic included). Seeing their faith, Jesus first addressed the man's spiritual needs. There are no formulas for the order in which needs are met: spiritual first and then physical, for the pattern varies. Jesus told the paralyzed man, "Friend, your sins are forgiven" (5:20). What a wonderful word to hear, *friend!* Jesus called him his friend. Then he said, "your sins are forgiven." I believe Jesus wants to say that to all of us.

Why were the teachers of the law and the Pharisees present? They often showed up to watch Jesus, to catch him doing something that was outside of their traditions. If they had seen him touch a leper, they would have howled, but they did hear him speak of forgiving some-one's sins. Their minds were having trouble digesting those words. Their unspoken questions are understand-able: *Who is Jesus and who can forgive sins?* Unfortunately they modified the questions to inwardly condemn Jesus for blasphemy and for doing something they reserved for God alone. In their understanding, the penalty for such blasphemy would be to have Jesus put to death.

Before these religious leaders could speak, Jesus did. "Why are you thinking these things in your hearts?" (5:22). He then gave them something to reflect on: which was easier, forgive the man's sins or perform a miracle of healing? Jesus implied that it was easier to say something than do it—easier to say *I forgive* rather than actually heal someone and enable them to walk. Jesus did not wait for reflection or answers from his critics. Instead he brought up the issue of authority. What authority did Jesus act upon? Earlier in Luke, we find Satan testing Jesus on the issue of authority (Luke 4:5–8). Jesus revealed his author-ity by saying "Worship the Lord your God and serve him only" (4:8). In the ministry that followed that time of test-ing, Jesus acted within the fullness of the authority of God. He obediently executed the mission of God. God gave him the power to both heal and forgive. To prove his point, Jesus brought forgiveness first to this man he would end up healing. He had the authority to do both. Jesus turned away from his critics and devoted his atten-tion to the man he would heal.

The paralyzed man had already heard the unexpected, that his sins were forgiven. Now Jesus told him to rise, walk, and go home. Note the man's response: he immediately stood up in front of Jesus' critics, his friends, and the crowd. He then took his mat and started walking home, praising God all the way. What a different trip than the one he made earlier in the day! Can you imagine the excitement of his friends? They had carried him to Jesus. They believed Jesus could help. Now they were walking home together!

What about the rest of the crowd? The critics were there, the committed were there, and probably the disciples as well. Luke does not differentiate between any of them, he simply writes that everyone was amazed and praised God. They were in awe of what must have been a holy moment. They said, "We have seen remarkable things today" (5:26). Perhaps this response could mean that even the critics gave Jesus some credit. The curious were amazed and Jesus' followers were strengthened.

Then and Now

Jesus was a miracle worker who healed many people. In varied circumstances, Jesus restored people to the way God intended them to be. Paralyzed people were created to walk, blind people to see, and deaf people to hear (see Matt. 11:4–6). Jesus was in the restoration business. Jesus was also in the redirection business. He had a purpose for those who were healed. When they left him they praised God because they had seen and experienced remarkable things. Their future was different because of Jesus.

Whether we suffer alone or within a caring community, we can know that God is not unconcerned about our struggle. God chooses to be there with us, helping to restore us to his ideal will and helping to redirect us to the good future he has for us. Sometimes, we have to walk a lonely path to Jesus; most often however, others are willing to walk with us. When heartaches come your way or when you may need healing of any sort, don't turn inward but look to Jesus. He will meet your need and he will provide people to help you when you cannot make your way to him alone. His healing touch is still available today.

PHARISEES

The Pharisees arose during the time between the Old and New Testaments. Initially they were a lay movement that helped Judaism survive the tough times of domination by foreign powers. By the time of Christ, they became a leading division within Judaism. The Pharisees appear frequently in the Gospels, fulfilling their self-appointed role as guardian of the faith and making sure that Jesus, a popular young teacher, was observing all the ways of the Jewish faith. As religious legalists, they came under severe criticism from Jesus (Luke 11:37–52). Luke wrote, "The Pharisees and the teachers of the law began to oppose him fiercely and to besiege him with questions, waiting to catch him in something he might say" (Luke 11:53–54). Their hostility toward Christians continued long after the resurrection of Jesus.

Saul was a famous Pharisee in the New Testament who was converted on his way to persecute Christians in Damascus (Acts 9:1–31). He became known as Paul, one of the first Christian missionaries and writer of many New Testament books.

GOING THROUGH THE ROOF TO REACH OUTCASTS

You are in charge of a missions committee in your church, with a specific assignment. Identify individuals or groups who are treated like outcasts. Bring a report to the church that includes: (1) attitudes toward these persons that need to change within your congregation, (2) practical ways of developing personal relationships with these persons, and (3) suggestions for how the church can go *through the roof* in bringing outcast and ignored people to God and to the fellowship of your church.

QUESTIONS

1. If you could ask God for healing of any kind, what would you ask for? What areas of your life need his healing touch?

2. The lepers of the first century were labeled as unclean or unfit for association with religious people. Who are those people in our culture or among your friends, neighbors, or co-workers?

3. How much time did you spend in prayer during the
   last week, just spending time alone with God? How
   could you adjust your schedule to spend more time
   with him?

4. If you and your Bible class were present the day the
   paralytic was healed, would your class members feel
   that your spirit was more like the critical Pharisees,
   the curious crowd, or the men who brought the
   paralytic to Jesus?

5. What is the most remarkable experience you have had with God? Who can you share it with?

6. What in this lesson helps you to prepare for Christmas?

NOTES ————————————————————————————

1. Unless otherwise indicated, all Scripture quotations in lessons 1–13 and the Christmas lesson are taken from the HOLY BIBLE, NEW INTERNATIONAL VERSION®. Copyright © 1973, 1978, 1984 Biblica.

LESSON TWO

A Humble Request and a Hopeless Situation

MAIN IDEA

Jesus granted the faithful request of a humble centurion and brought a miraculous remedy to a hopeless widow.

QUESTION TO EXPLORE

How can we demonstrate faith in Jesus in the midst of hopeless situations?

STUDY AIM

To identify hopeless situations in my life and to describe how I will respond to them with faith in Jesus

QUICK READ

In light of Jesus' miracles for persons and families in great distress, we can know that God will help us face the difficult challenges of life with hope and faith.

We do not need much training in how to ask for something. At first the request might not be verbal, but even a baby communicates well when things go wrong. In today's Scripture, we see an unusual request from a group of Jews who asked Jesus to help a non-Jew, an officer of the occupying Roman army. We read about the remarkable faith of this man, known as a centurion. Even Jesus marveled at what he said. Following this account, Jesus saw a grieving woman whose only son had died. She was on the way to the graveyard with his body. Jesus was moved with compassion for the woman. In these two miraculous events, Jesus revealed his power over death. He could prevent it, as in the case of the centurion's servant; and he could also overcome it, as with the widow's son. Jesus responded to the requests and faith of people who were in great need.

LUKE 7:1–17

[1] When Jesus had finished saying all this in the hearing of the people, he entered Capernaum. [2] There a centurion's servant, whom his master valued highly, was sick and about to die. [3] The centurion heard of Jesus and sent some elders of the Jews to him, asking him to come and heal his servant. [4] When they came to Jesus, they pleaded earnestly with him, "This man deserves to have you do this, [5] because he loves our nation and has built

our synagogue." **6** So Jesus went with them. He was not far from the house when the centurion sent friends to say to him: "Lord, don't trouble yourself, for I do not deserve to have you come under my roof. **7** That is why I did not even consider myself worthy to come to you. But say the word, and my servant will be healed. **8**For I myself am a man under authority, with soldiers under me. I tell this one, 'Go,' and he goes; and that one, 'Come,' and he comes. I say to my servant, 'Do this,' and he does it." **9** When Jesus heard this, he was amazed at him, and turning to the crowd following him, he said, "I tell you, I have not found such great faith even in Israel." **10** Then the men who had been sent returned to the house and found the servant well. **11** Soon afterward, Jesus went to a town called Nain, and his disciples and a large crowd went along with him. **12** As he approached the town gate, a dead person was being carried out—the only son of his mother, and she was a widow. And a large crowd from the town was with her. **13** When the Lord saw her, his heart went out to her and he said, "Don't cry." **14** Then he went up and touched the coffin, and those carrying it stood still. He said, "Young man, I say to you, get up!"**15** The dead man sat up and began to talk, and Jesus gave him back to his mother. **16** They were all filled with awe and praised God. "A great prophet has appeared among us," they said. "God has come to help his people." **17** This news about Jesus spread throughout Judea and the surrounding country.

When People Ask Jesus for Help (7:1–5)

Capernaum was the center of Jesus' ministry in Galilee. Located on the northwestern shore of the Sea of Galilee, Jesus spent much time there. In Luke 4:31–44, Jesus healed a man in the synagogue and then went to Simon Peter's home and healed his mother-in-law. Afterward, many others sought to be healed by Jesus. When Jesus returned to Capernaum in Luke 7, people remembered him. So did a Roman official who asked some citizens of Capernaum for help.

The Roman official was both a Gentile and a centurion, a leading official of the occupying government. Centurions were normally in charge of at least 100 soldiers, stationed to protect tax collectors and keep order. In a rare occurrence, the elders of the city, who may also have been synagogue leaders, sought out Jesus on behalf of the centurion. Generally, Jews did not care for centurions but this centurion was an exception to the norm.

The centurion's servant was at the point of death. The term *servant* may be a kind translation, for persons like him were really slaves. Slavery in those days was based on economics, not race. Sometimes the slaves of centurions actually fought on behalf of their owners and/or served as their personal attendants or house slaves. Though a slave had economic value, the story indicates that the centurion genuinely cared about his servant/slave. Several translations use the word *dear* to describe how the centurion felt about him. That was an unusual description for a master/ slave relationship.

The centurion asked the elders of the Jews to contact Jesus on his behalf. He truly believed that Jesus could heal his servant. When the Jewish men found Jesus, they spoke fondly and appreciatively of the centurion. They believed he was worthy of a miracle. Specifically, they told Jesus that the centurion loved their nation and had built their synagogue. The centurion may have donated money or helped construct the synagogue. We do not know exactly how he helped build the synagogue, but he was well-respected by the Jews of Capernaum. Jesus accepted their invitation and walked with them toward the centurion's house.

The example of the elders challenges us. Perhaps you have a prayer list and you intercede regularly for others. That is good, but how faithful are you in performing *intercessory ministry* to others? You might not be able to walk with them to Jesus, but you can do something that helps connect someone to Jesus or minister to them in his name. Be intentional, act on purpose for the good of someone else, including those who may not be some of your best friends.

Amazing Faith (7:6–10)

Luke does not indicate that Jesus actually arrived at the centurion's home. On the way there, the centurion sent some more friends to speak to Jesus. He did not want Jesus to travel any farther. He did not feel worthy of Jesus entering his home. The centurion may have respected Jewish tradition and did not want Jesus to become defiled by entering a Gentile house. Jesus would not be concerned about that, but some of those who were watching Jesus were keenly aware of such things. Regardless, the centurion was humble, disclaiming any sense of worthiness on his part. That may be why he did not go directly to Jesus, but asked others to go on his behalf. His interest in Jesus was not based on anything related to his position or self-worth as a centurion; it was based on what he thought about Jesus.

Jesus responded to the servant's need when he heard of the centurion's great faith. His faith was expressed in terms of authority. The centurion understood authority, for he was under authority, probably representing Herod Antipas. He also exercised authority. When he spoke, people listened and acted. The centurion recognized Jesus as a person under authority and as one who possessed authority. From what he had seen and heard about Jesus, he believed that all Jesus needed to do was say the word and his servant would be healed.

Jesus described the centurion's faith as "great" (7:9) and said he had not seen such faith in all of Israel. Jesus did not disparage the faith of the Jews or even his disciples, but he was amazed at what he heard from the centurion. Certainly, he had seen people exercise faith.

Jesus performed miracles for those who deeply believed in him. Some left their fishing business to follow Jesus and his disciples. One left his position as tax collector to follow Jesus. Other followers had made sacrifices and commitments, but this Gentile centurion received one of the greatest compliments for his faith. When the friends returned to the centurion's house, they found the servant had been healed! What an experience that must have been for the elders of the city as well as the friends of the centurion.

A Heartfelt Healing (7:11–17)

Both Scripture and experience teach us to do the right thing because it is the right thing to do. Don't wait around for emotion or attention, just do the right thing. However, we also know the value of emotion and compassion. We cannot go through life with filters in our mind that cause us to shut out those less fortunate, or to ignore the pain of others. Demonstrating grace and mercy is often part of doing the right thing.

Nain was on the southwest side of the Sea of Galilee, not far from Jesus' hometown of Nazareth. The disciples and many others traveled with Jesus. As they approached the town, they saw a funeral procession. Luke was blunt, "a dead person was being carried out" (7:12). Jesus and his friends realized there was more to this story; the mother of the dead person was a widow and the coffin contained her only son. The son may have been her joy in life and was probably the primary means of her financial support. Interestingly, nothing is said of her faith, but the Scripture records that "when the Lord saw her, his heart went out to her" (7:13). Jesus was moved with compassion. He hurt for her, he hurt with her. Then Jesus said, "Don't cry" (7:13).

Normally it is okay to cry. Jesus' command is not for every circumstance or time. Jesus himself wept and sometimes we do also. Jesus did not just say "don't cry" nor did he wipe away her tears. He took away the reason for her tears. Jesus broke tradition again, he touched the coffin. This act would have defiled him in Jewish eyes, but Jesus knew the fruitlessness of so much of their tradition. Jesus spoke to the dead man, saying "Young man, I say to you, get up!" (7:14). Then the corpse began to talk and "Jesus gave him back to his mother" (7:15). What a beautiful line! What a gift!

The healing of the widow's son made an impact on others as well. The people were awed by what happened. Luke records responses that reflect the Old Testament traditions that had become part of the everyday lore of the people. The saying "a great prophet has appeared among us" may go back to the ministry of both Elijah (1 Kings 17:17–24) and Elisha (2 Kings 4:8–37). In the Elijah account, the son of a widow in Sidon died and Elijah cried out to God, "let this boy's life return to him!" (1 Kings 17:21). God answered Elijah's prayer and Elijah carried the boy to his mother, telling her "your son is alive!" (17:23). Both Elijah and Elisha were Jews who were recognized as great prophets, and in Nain some were applying that title to Jesus. From the Exodus onward, the people were accustomed to hearing and saying that *God has come to help his people*. Those who witnessed the healing of the widow's son or heard about it may not have known that Jesus was God in human flesh, but they believed God was doing something wonderful through him.

Jesus often had custom instructions for those he healed. He did not use the opportunity to promote himself as a folk hero who was a miracle worker. On some occasions, Jesus told those he healed to tell no one, but some did not follow his instructions. Apparently, their miracle was such good news they had to share it. On other occasions, nothing was instructed, but the word circulated anyway. In a world without mass media or modern communication abilities, apparently people just told one another, and amazingly, "news about Jesus spread" (Luke 7:17). That is a word of encouragement for us today. It still matters when one person tells another person about what Jesus has done in his or her life.

The New Testament mentions three instances when Jesus raised someone from the dead. In addition to the widow's son, Jesus raised the daughter of Jairus (Luke 8:40–56) and Lazarus of Bethany (John 11:1–45). The widow's son had been dead less than a day, Jairus's daughter only a few minutes, and Lazarus for about four days.

Jesus not only had the ability to stop the disease that would lead to death, he also had the power to overcome death. Jesus literally brought life from death; foreshadowing what would happen to him between Good Friday and Easter Sunday.

Jesus truly had a heart for people. He saw people as valuable simply because they existed. He dealt with people according to their individual needs. He felt compassion for people, but he did not substitute warm emotion for action. His compassion was accompanied by a love that acted for the betterment of others. Even today, we are challenged to have the heart of Jesus as we seek to minister and witness to others.

Hope for Today

If we live long enough, each of us will be like the prophetic description of the Messiah: "a man of sorrows, and familiar with suffering" (Isa. 53:3). Christian or atheist, rich or poor, any ethnic or racial distinction, male or female; name the category, we all deal with tough times in life.

Jesus is our source of hope for seemingly hopeless situations. He continues to offer holy compassion and supernatural strength to those who trust in him. Jesus answered the prayers of a Roman soldier and a grieving widow. He brought hope, healing, and life to those afflicted. He still does that today. Healing still happens and faith still matters. Even if we do not get our health restored or our prayers answered as we would like, God will give us miracles of grace and strength to deal positively with whatever we face (Phil. 4:19). With God, life is never hopeless. In the end, God, not the coroner, has the last word. Paul reminds us that nothing in death or life will ever separate us from the love of God in Christ Jesus our Lord (Rom. 8:38–39).

THE GOSPEL FOR ALL PEOPLE

At Jesus' birth, the angel spoke of "good news of great joy that will be for all the people" (Luke 2:10). Luke had a special interest in showing the *whosoever will* nature of the mission and ministry of Jesus. Jesus ministered, taught, and associated lovingly with Jews, Gentiles, tax collectors, the poor, the rich, religious leaders, and those on the fringes of society. His love touched all people. He stepped over traditional boundaries. As in all things, Jesus is our model.

Luke continues the theme of God's love for all people in the Book of Acts, his second volume. In Acts 1:6–8, Jesus commissioned the disciples to take the gospel to Samaria and to the uttermost parts of the earth. Later, Peter and Paul embraced the universal mission of the gospel. Peter figured prominently in the conversion of a non-Jew, Cornelius (Acts 10:34), and Paul's missionary work (Acts

13:1–3) eventually took him to Rome. Not only was the gospel extended to all people, Christians were to have fellowship and do ministry with them as well (Acts 15).

WHEN RELATIONSHIPS NEED HEALING

Notice five truths from the stories of the centurion and grieving widow. Assume you have a serious relationship problem with an older child or friend that has persisted for several years. How can these principles change your attitude and behavior toward this person?

- Jesus is compassionate and caring about the issues we face

- You can find support from friends and family in difficult times

- You can exercise faith that God can heal broken relationships

- You can initiate the healing process by taking the first step to mend the relationship

- Sometimes our prayers are answered in marvelous ways, but sometimes we have the opportunity to grow in our faith as we wait

QUESTIONS

1. When a friend faces a difficult situation, perhaps one that appears hopeless, how can you encourage that person to respond with faith in Jesus? What acts of ministry could you offer?

2. How does your faith in Jesus enable you to deal more positively with the tough circumstances you face?

3. Are you talking with Jesus about your family members or friends who are facing adversity? Are you practicing the ministry of presence with them?

4. What is the relationship between suffering and sin?

5. If anyone saw your checkbook or documented how you spend your time, would they think you were living according to the authority and will of God?

FOCAL TEXT

Luke 10:25–37

BACKGROUND

Luke 10:21–37

LESSON THREE

Love Without Limits

MAIN IDEA

Jesus used the parable of the Good Samaritan to destroy accepted boundaries of love expressed through service to others.

QUESTION TO EXPLORE

What are the motives behind the limits you place on your love and service to others?

STUDY AIM

To recognize the motives that influence my love and service for others, and to commit to following Jesus' teaching on servanthood

QUICK READ

Christlike love does not seek limits; it recognizes opportunities to help and then acts to make the lives of others better.

Why did I do that? Most of us have asked that question, sometimes others ask it of us. Occasionally, our answers reveal something weak or wrong about our motives. On other occasions, someone might ask us how we were able to handle a difficult situation. Such questions provide us an opportunity to express our faith. For most of us, motives are often a mixed bag. Sometimes we do things for the right reasons and at other times we demonstrate selfishness. Today's lesson is about a man who did good things. Perhaps it was all he knew how to do, but Jesus challenged him concerning the attitudes behind his actions. In the process, Jesus gave us one of his most famous parables, the story of the Good Samaritan.

LUKE 10:25–37

25 On one occasion an expert in the law stood up to test Jesus. "Teacher," he asked, "what must I do to inherit eternal life?" **26** "What is written in the Law?" he replied. "How do you read it?" **27** He answered: "'Love the Lord your God with all your heart and with all your soul and with all your strength and with all your mind'; and, 'Love your neighbor as yourself.'" **28** "You have answered correctly," Jesus replied. "Do this and you will live." **29** But he wanted to justify himself, so he asked Jesus, "And who is my neighbor?" **30** In reply Jesus said: "A man was going down from Jerusalem to Jericho, when he fell into the hands of robbers. They stripped him of his clothes, beat him and went away, leaving him half dead. **31** A priest happened to be going down the same road, and when he saw the man, he passed by on the other side. **32** So too, a Levite, when he came to the place and saw him, passed by on the other side. **33** But a Samaritan, as he traveled, came where the man was; and when he saw him, he took pity on him. **34** He went to him and bandaged his wounds, pouring on oil and wine. Then he put the man on his own donkey, took him to an inn and took care of him. **35** The next day he took out two silver coins and gave them to the innkeeper. 'Look after him,' he said, 'and when I return, I will reimburse you for any extra expense you may have.' **36** "Which of these three do you think was a neighbor to the man who fell into the hands of robbers?" **37** The expert in the law replied, "The one who had mercy on him." Jesus told him, "Go and do likewise."

The Setting of the Parable (10:25–29)

Those opposed to the popular teacher from Nazareth often tried to catch Jesus doing or saying something wrong. On one occasion, "an expert in the law" (Luke 10:25) tried to do that. His expertise was not the law in a judicial sense, but in the Old Testament law and in the commentaries made on it over the passing of time. He thought he was testing Jesus, but Jesus quickly turned the lawyer's words into a test of the lawyer.

The lawyer's question was a good one for someone with his background. He had been trained to understand that the way to be made right with God was to *do* many things. Such training was the orientation of the Jewish religion. Eternal life is mentioned often in the Gospel of John during Jesus' ministry in Jerusalem and Judea, but not in the other Gospels. Jesus accepts the man's terms for discussion, but rather than giving an answer, Jesus asked him a question concerning his understanding of the law.

Jesus' query could have opened the door for much information; however, the lawyer briefly summarized the Ten Commandments. The first part of his answer was from the Shema of Deuteronomy 6:5, which focuses on our love of God and summarizes the first four commandments. The second came out of the Holiness Code of Leviticus 19:18, which deals with loving your neighbor as yourself, and summarizes the other six commandments. In Matthew 22:34–40, these two Scriptures are referred to as The Great Commandment, which we often summarize as *love God and love neighbor.* The lawyer answered correctly and Jesus commended him for it. However, Jesus knew that seemingly wise people may have *book knowledge* about truth but lack the *heart knowledge* to apply it properly (see Luke 10:21).

The lawyer continued the discussion, wanting to justify himself and perhaps look even better in the eyes of Jesus and the others. His question opens the door for a probing of his life and continues to challenge ours as well. "Who is my neighbor?" (10:29). The lawyer felt no need to address the first object of love, God himself; however, identifying the neighbor was important to him. The lawyer's question led to a story that went straight to the lawyer's heart. It also speaks to the nature of love. The lawyer was looking for limits, boundaries, and loopholes. As a person obsessed with rules and legalistic precision, he was not looking for expanded opportunities to be a neighbor, but for ways to avoid being involved with some people. That sort of attitude is not what love is about. True love seeks and responds to opportunities of service.

Characters in the Parable of the Good Samaritan (10:30–35)

One definition of a parable is that it is *an earthly story with a heavenly meaning.* Parables dealt with life that people understood; such as sowing seeds in a field, catching fish, or building a house. Jesus used these short stories to help people grasp deeper truths about God and themselves. In the Good Samaritan story, people could visualize the road from Jerusalem to Jericho. They knew it was a tough twenty mile trip through rugged terrain and dangerous territory.

Many priests and others made the trip to and from Jerusalem often. Some unknown person is the first character, falling victim to robbers. Jesus' audience understood that possibility. The first person to arrive on the scene was a priest. He might not have wanted to become ceremonially defiled by dealing with such a problem on the way home from doing religious work. He may have served God for a normal shift in the temple of seven days; now he had a chance to serve man. The second was a Levite, a temple employee who had liturgical responsibilities and took care of the temple. Like the priest, he too passed by on the other side. Both saw the victim, both chose to keep walking and do nothing to help a fellow Jew in need. The priest and the Levite were motivated by religious rules, and when challenged by human need, the rules won. Neither person had compassion for someone in a life-or-death situation. Could the lawyer have seen himself in the priest and Levite? Could you?

Then a Samaritan showed up. Samaritans were despised by Jews, dating from centuries earlier when Jews in the Northern Kingdom of Israel married non-Jewish persons who had conquered them. They were unaffectionately known as *half-breeds*. Jesus said that the Samaritan "saw him" and "took pity on him" (10:33). He saw the man and stopped walking. He felt sorry for him and did not leave him on the side of the road. He performed all the first-aid he could for the man. He then put him on his donkey, took him to an inn and cared for him. The Samaritan also had

LESSON 3: *Love Without Limits*   59

other things to do, but on the next day, he paid the innkeeper and asked him to look out for the wounded man
until he returned. He promised to reimburse him for any
additional expense. Though Jews typically did not have
anything to do with Samaritans, the innkeeper agreed.

The priest, the Levite, and the Samaritan were not
looking for problems. They were simply travelers who
came upon a problem. The King James Version says about
the priest and Levite that they came upon this man "by
chance" (10:31). Sometimes that is the way life is. It just
happens. We do not plan for it, but when life unfolds in
front of us, we are called to respond. The priest and Levite
responded; they walked by on the other side. They passed
by someone who needed help. It was also "by chance" that
the Samaritan was there as well. His presence mattered
and it was his presence in the story that would startle the
Jewish listeners.

The Samaritan, as the unlikely hero of the story, is part
of Luke's continuing purpose to show Jesus as the Savior
for all people. The sad part of the story is that the priest
and Levite represented organized religion; people who
professionally and personally were called to be good (and
to do good), but chose not to. In contrast, the Samaritan
represented persons who were outcasts of Jewish society.
If we were to paraphrase this story today, we might make
the hero anyone who represents a group of people whom
many dislike and look down upon. Lest we be too hard on
the lawyer, priest, or Levite, we might examine ourselves

to see if we have negative attitudes about people who are different from us.

Don't forget the victim. He too was traveling "by chance." He traveled the dangerous road just like anyone else; however, bandits beat him and robbed him. Fortunately, most of us have not had that happen to us. You may know persons who have experienced that tragedy or have experienced life in such a way that they feel emotionally stripped and battered. If so, don't pass them by. Reach out to them. You can become Christ or the church to others when you minister to them in their time of need.

One other group is also present, the robbers. Our world has many people who rob and terrorize others. News reports give daily evidence of the crimes that such persons commit. Rarely will you ever hear or read that these people sinned, but they have. Don't ignore the spiritual needs of robbers. Their actions hurt people and are an affront to God. Robbers are villains in the story, though in some ways, the priest and Levite are just as bad as the thieves. The thieves ganged up on a solitary traveler. Those who thought they represented God ignored the wounded person. We must not compound the misery of those abused and harmed by failing to act to help them in their time of great need. For additional study on seeing needs and responding in service, read Jesus' parable on life's final exam in Matthew 25:31–46.

The Conclusion of the Test (10:36–37)

The encounter began with the lawyer trying to test Jesus, wanting to know what he had to do to earn eternal life. It continued with the lawyer wanting to define who his neighbor was. It concludes with Jesus changing the emphasis. Jesus answered the lawyer's question in verse 29—a neighbor is anyone who needs your love and mercy. When Jesus asked the lawyer which person proved to be the neighbor to the man, he answered correctly, "the one who had mercy on him" (10:37). Interestingly, the lawyer chose not to use the word *Samaritan*. His prejudice would not allow him to acknowledge out loud that the hated Samaritan was the hero.

Jesus ended the conversation with a call to decision and action. The issue was no longer about who the lawyer's neighbor was, nor who proved to be a neighbor. The issue was the lawyer himself. If the lawyer was truly looking for the most complete life, one that God would bless, Jesus told him to "go and do likewise" (10:37). Though he was Jewish, he was to follow the example of the Good Samaritan.

The lawyer finally got his answer to the *do* question, "What must I do to inherit eternal life?" (10:25). The *do* answer was not an answer that would bring salvation to the lawyer. That's another issue. What the lawyer needed to *do* was to love God and love his neighbor. He was to personalize that love by seeing people's needs as a call to serve. Have you ever bumped into someone and one of you said, "I'm sorry, I didn't see you." That's understandable, but at a deeper level, how well do we see people? Are there people in need that we intentionally avoid?

The lawyer had a great need: he needed to see people with his eyes and his heart, and then act like the Samaritan. Jesus wanted the lawyer to be moved emotionally by the needs of others and do something about them. The Samaritan did, and that's a good model for us as well.

Another Great Commission for Today

Bible students are familiar with the last words of Matthew 28. Those words are Jesus' marching orders to the church to make disciples to the end of the earth. We call that *The Great Commission.* The four Gospels and the Book of Acts contain some version of this mandate for the church to fulfill in the world. In today's Scripture, we have another Great Commission. It is the commission to "go and do likewise" (Luke 10:37). Do not hesitate when it comes to compassionate action. Jesus commanded it. *Go,* whether it is by chance or by intention. *Do,* try to meet the needs of hurting people.

Where are we to go and what are are we to do? As we go into the world, we can accept people as neighbors and try to be good neighbors to them. Like the Good Samaritan, we can truly see people, be soft-hearted enough to feel the pain and sorrow of others, and be willing to adjust our schedules to help those in need. We can serve hurting people, including opening our wallets to them. We then can follow-up in ways that are appropriate to the needs of the person. Does that describe you?

FEELINGS AND COMMANDS

The priest and Levite appeared insensitive to the needs of a beaten man. The Samaritan saw the same scene, but felt differently: "he took pity on him" (Luke 10:33). We deal with the same issues as these three persons: we are prompted by feelings and we are given commands.

Feelings and commands can reveal our love for God and our neighbor, but what is love? The Greeks had four words for love: one for our love for God (*agape*); others for friendly love, romantic love, and family love. When the lawyer said we should love God and love our neighbors, the word for love is *agape*, a Godly love that seeks to do the best for others. That love is made bigger by compassion, but it does not depend on emotions. We are commanded to demonstrate *agape* love whether we feel like it or not. Such love does not seek to limit our responsibilities to others, but serves people just as Christ would.

Are you a command person or a feeling person? You can be both.

THE GOOD SAMARITAN ATTITUDE

Within Jesus' parable, we find three attitudes toward people in need:

- What is yours is mine, and I am going to take it.

- What is mine is mine, and I am going to keep it.

- What is mine is ours, and I am going to share it.

Examine your use of time and money to see if you exhibit a Good Samaritan mindset toward those in need. When it comes to organizations that help people or individuals in need, keep in mind that you can be the answer to someone's prayer. Obey Jesus, be a Good Samaritan.

QUESTIONS

1. Who have been Good Samaritans to you? Have you thanked them lately?

2. What more can your class do together that expresses compassion and practical help for those in need?

3. With whom do you identify in this story: victim, priest, Levite, or Samaritan?

4. Would "Samaritans" (those on the fringe of society, different from regular members) feel comfortable in your church or class?

5. What is the difference in the following questions: (a) What must I do to inherit eternal life? and (b) What must I do to be saved?

6. To whom will you make an intentional effort to be a Good Samaritan?

FOCAL TEXT

Luke 12:13–34

BACKGROUND

Luke 11:53—12:59

LESSON FOUR

Greed vs. Need

MAIN IDEA

Jesus contrasted the danger of greed with the generous provision of God to meet our needs.

QUESTION TO EXPLORE

Are we greedy, or are we trusting God to meet our needs?

STUDY AIM

To evaluate my attitude toward my wealth and possessions and to commit to being a faithful steward who trusts God to meet my needs.

QUICK READ

Jesus demonstrated the consequences of two distinct attitudes towards our money and possessions— the danger of greed and the generous provision of God.

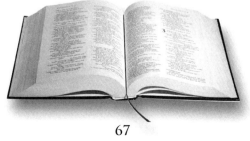

My car still had that new car smell. The Toyota® Camry couldn't have been more than two weeks old when I drove it up to the stoplight. As I glanced to my left, I spotted her pulling up right next to me. "She" was a Lexus® GS300 and in the fad color of the day—forest green. The car was both sporty and elegant.

My imagination went wild in the brief moment that I waited for the stoplight to turn green. How would I look driving a car like that? I couldn't imagine a smoother ride. I could almost feel the smoothness of the leather seats. Then it hit me.

No, it wasn't a car that rear-ended me while my day-dreaming continued at the red light. What hit me was the truth—the truth of the greed I was experiencing. I immediately felt embarrassed and had to confess my greed. *Lord, here I am sitting in a brand new car and instead of being thankful, I'm envying the car next to me. I'm sorry.*

Unfortunately, that was not the first time I had to adjust my attitude about my stuff. And it wasn't the last. Is this struggle an all too familiar experience for you as well? In the parable of the Rich Fool, Jesus shows us how to overcome an attitude of greed by placing our trust in the generous provision of God.

LUKE 12:13–34

13 Someone in the crowd said to him, "Teacher, tell my brother to divide the inheritance with me."14 Jesus replied, "Man, who appointed me a judge or an arbiter between you?" 15 Then he said to them, "Watch out! Be on your guard against all kinds of greed; a man's life does not consist in the abundance of his possessions." 16 And he told them this parable: "The ground of a certain rich man produced a good crop. 17 He thought to himself, 'What shall I do? I have no place to store my crops.' 18 "Then he said, 'This is what I'll do. I will tear down my barns and build bigger ones, and there I will store all my grain and my goods. 19 And I'll say to myself, "You have plenty of good things laid up for many years. Take life easy; eat, drink and be merry."' 20 "But God said to him, 'You fool! This very night your life will be demanded from you. Then who will get what you have prepared for yourself ?' 21 "This is how it will be with anyone who stores up things for himself but is not rich toward God." 22 Then Jesus said to his disciples: "Therefore I tell you, do not worry about your life, what you will eat; or about your body, what you will wear. 23 Life is more than food, and the body more than clothes. 24 Consider the ravens: They do not sow or reap, they have no storeroom or barn; yet God feeds them. And how much more valuable you are than birds! 25 Who of you by worrying can add a single hour to his life? 26 Since you cannot do this very little thing, why do

you worry about the rest? **27** "Consider how the lilies grow. They do not labor or spin. Yet I tell you, not even Solomon in all his splendor was dressed like one of these. **28** If that is how God clothes the grass of the field, which is here today, and tomorrow is thrown into the fire, how much more will he clothe you, O you of little faith! **29** And do not set your heart on what you will eat or drink; do not worry about it. **30** For the pagan world runs after all such things, and your Father knows that you need them. **31** But seek his kingdom, and these things will be given to you as well. **32** "Do not be afraid, little flock, for your Father has been pleased to give you the kingdom. **33** Sell your possessions and give to the poor. Provide purses for yourselves that will not wear out, a treasure in heaven that will not be exhausted, where no thief comes near and no moth destroys. **34** For where your treasure is, there your heart will be also.

A Look At Our Hands Reveals Our Hearts (12:13–14)

With no small claims courts or Judge Judy to decide such disputes, it was not uncommon for someone to look to a rabbi such as Jesus to settle an inheritance or property dispute. No doubt the man had spent much time debating his brother over the division of the inheritance. Perhaps even family members and neighbors had unwittingly been brought into the dispute. Now the brother chooses to present his case in the court of public opinion. In front of friends and neighbors he yells out "Teacher, tell my brother to divide the inheritance with me" (Luke 12:13).

Jesus understood that the man's request to settle the property dispute was just a symptom of the real, underlying problem. The man's words couldn't help but reveal his motives. "For out of the overflow of his heart his mouth speaks" (Luke 6:45). Even a rightful division of the inheritance would not have resolved the brother's real problem—the motivation of his heart. The brother could have in his hands the inheritance he thought he deserved, but what would be in his hands would not change his heart.

Knowing that the brother was not the only one in the crowd facing the same battle within, Jesus addressed the crowd. His first words were telling—"Watch out!" (12:15) This was not a casual recommendation.

"Watch out!" is the kind of phrase you yell at someone who is about to get knocked out by a speeding baseball. They are the kind of words that you yell when someone is about to step in front of a car that is barreling down the street. Jesus described an impending danger that required action on the part of all those who heard his warning. "Be on your guard against all kinds of greed" (12:15). This simple statement revealed two powerful truths about greed.

First, we know that we can be on our guard. We don't have to sit idly by while greed attacks. Jesus challenges us to participate in our own defense. Be on guard. As we stand guard, what are some tell-tale signs that the threat of greed is near? Look for those things that are exhausting too much of your attention. Am I spending an inordinate amount of time fretting over possessions, bills, or money? What has been the center of my focus? Is it that I can't stop turning my neck every time I see a particular make and model of truck? Do I find myself daydreaming about what it would be like to own that "must-have" item I saw advertised?

The more I am on guard against greed, the more I become acquainted with its tactics. Greed can creep into our thoughts, consume our idle moments, and begin to take over our energies. We can soon find ourselves in the grip of greed. What we long to possess in our hands, soon possesses us.

What is in your hands? What is it that your hands work so hard for? What do they long to hold? A look at your hands may give a revealing view of what is deep down in your heart.

The second truth reveals the diversity of our threat in "all kinds of greed" (12:15). Greed is usually understood to be an unhealthy or excessive desire to acquire money or possessions. However, greed isn't limited to the kind depicted in the caricature of the insanely wealthy Wall Street banker, consumed with passion for acquiring more money at any cost. While this may be one kind of greed, it is not the only example.

A poor person accuses a wealthy person of being greedy in regard to tax breaks. A wealthy person may accuse a poor person of being greedy for government entitlements. The reality is that you can be rich, poor, or middle-class and still be greedy. I can and you can too.

You Are Not Your Stuff (12:15)

Jesus followed his "watch out" warning with a liberating declaration that "a man's life does not consist in the abundance of his possessions" (Luke 12:15b). You are not the sum of your stuff.

For a while I drove a pickup truck that was old, had no air-conditioning, and had an awful paint job. I recall pulling into a parking spot about the same time as a brand new truck. The paint job on the new truck was impeccable. The technology was the latest, and the chrome was shiny. The owner proudly got out and declared his arrival with a quick press of the alarm button. Wow, even the "beep" announcing that the alarm was armed was bold, bright, and very manly.

I couldn't help feeling as we walked through the parking lot, that we did so as walking reflections of what we were driving. He walked boldly and confidently in a "shiny new-truck" kind of way. I felt as if I lumbered on in more of a "clunker truck" fashion.

Neither of us would trade our lives for our trucks. Both of us would have to leave them behind after we died. The trucks were equally valueless when compared to the important things in our lives—faith, family, and love. Both would be useless on our deathbed. Why then do we so often let such things define who we are, how we're perceived, or what we believe we're worth? More importantly, how do we change our attitude about what we own?

The Foolishness of Misplaced Trust (12:16–21)

Rarely is faith theoretical. Biblical truth always intersects life with clear consequences. Jesus illustrated how the threat of greed plays out in real life through the story of a wealthy farmer.

Jesus tells us the farmer was wealthy, but does not indicate that God had a problem with the farmer's wealth. The farmer had a bumper crop. Again, the passage gives us no indication that Jesus felt there was something wrong with a well-off farmer having a bountiful harvest. The harvest was so fruitful, the farmer laid out a plan to tear down his existing barns and replace them with larger barns that were capable of holding his surplus grain. Still, the passage doesn't indicate that the farmer had done anything wrong in addressing either his harvest or his storage plans.

The farmer then said to himself, "You have plenty of good things laid up for many years. Take life easy; eat, drink and be merry" (12:19). Could the problem lie in the eating, drinking, and merriment? Again, this doesn't appear to be a problem. Ecclesiastes 3:13 tells us that to eat, drink, and find satisfaction in our work "is the gift of God." But we know the farmer in the parable did in fact have a problem. And you know it's a serious problem when God himself examines your circumstances and declares, "You fool!" (12:20).

The farmer's problem was not his hope for the future, but the *source* of hope for his future. He gazed at the grain. It was good. It was plentiful. And it evoked in him a comfort that assured him of a future life of ease filled with food, drink, and celebration. The problem was clear. It wasn't the fruitful surplus of grain. It was the foolish security placed in the grain. When we gaze on God and gain hope for our future we are being obedient. When we look to anything else for that assurance, we are being idolatrous.

"You fool! This very night your life will be demanded from you. Then who will get what you have prepared for yourself?" (12:20). The sun would set and all would be lost. The farmer would breathe his last breath. His life would be gone and his grain would remain. Left for some unknown someone to care for and manage.

Such is the reality of a manager. You get to oversee the estate, administer, invest, and reap the reward, but only while it is entrusted to you. The owner *owns*. The steward *stewards*. Foolishness arises when the steward begins to think of himself as the owner. Destructive foolishness arises when the steward places his hope in that which he does not own. Death was the sad result of the steward's misplaced trust. "This is how it will be with anyone who stores up things for himself but is not rich toward God" (12:21).

The Power of the Promise of Provision (12:22–34)

We spend a great amount of time working. We spend most of the pay from our work on food, shelter, and clothing. Jesus challenged the disciples "do not set your heart on what you will eat or drink; do not worry about it" (12:29). We are told "the pagan world runs after all such things" (12:30). The godless pursue *things* because, like the parable's farmer, they expect that *things* will bring them security, hope, or fulfillment.

"But seek his kingdom, and these things will be given to you as well" (12:31). The godly pursue his kingdom and its fulfillment. In doing so, the needs of this life will be met. Pursuing God's kingdom seems like an exhausting and overwhelming task. But we are encouraged, "Do not be afraid, little flock, for your Father has been pleased to give you the kingdom" (12:32). If he has already given you the kingdom, you can rest assured that he will readily give you what you need to meet your needs.

Applying This Truth in My Life

An attitude of greed is revealed in my life when the things I possess begin to possess me. The threat of greed increases when I begin to trust that my possessions will bring me security, hope, or happiness. When I recognize misplaced trust in my life, I can shift that trust to its rightful place— God's promise of provision. In doing so, I am freed to focus on pursuing his kingdom first. I can trust God to provide for my needs.

END OF GREED

Imagine "a world where poverty has ended and all people enjoy the fullness of life God intends." That is the vision of Australian Baptist World Aid (ABWA). ABWA is a Christian aid and development organization whose guiding principles are the Christian Scriptures. Their work begins in Baptist churches where they partner in areas including generous giving and ethical consumption. The ABWA then extends out to help empower communities so they can raise themselves out of poverty. Their resources for churches, including the "End of Greed" Bible study, are available free for download at www.baptistworldaid.org.au. The ABWA is one of many Baptist groups and churches that are actively being on guard against all kinds of greed and trusting in God for his provision. We can do the same.

ON GUARD AGAINST GREED

Take the following quiz to see if you are on guard against greed:

- Have I been increasing my use of credit cards or loans? This may be a sign that my spending is being controlled by my greed, rather than my budget.

- Am I spending more time "just looking" at the mall, through sales flyers, or browsing online stores?

- Have I resisted giving to others because I was worried about having enough for myself?

- List the top three money or material items you have been worried about. Pray about them and confess your trust in God to meet your needs.

QUESTIONS

1. If you were to remake this parable, what profession would the Rich Fool have in your modern day adaptation? How would the story play out?

2. What warning signs help you to be on guard against greed?

3. What different types of greed have you seen in others? In yourself?

4. How have you seen people define themselves by their possessions?

5. How could you be "rich towards God" this week?

6. What will you trust God to provide for you today?

FOCAL TEXT
Luke 13:10–17

BACKGROUND
Luke 13:10–17

LESSON FIVE

Focused on People, Not Rules

MAIN IDEA

Jesus healed a woman on the Sabbath and exposed the hypocritical hearts of those who valued rules more than people.

QUESTION TO EXPLORE

In what ways do we use our preconceived notions about faith to excuse us from meeting the needs of others?

STUDY AIM

To take the initiative in meeting the needs of others by overcoming my preconceived notions about how, when, and where God works

QUICK READ

Jesus healed a woman, but his miracle fell outside the comfort zone of the religious leaders. He addressed the attitude of the heart that values rules more than people.

The small church had decided it was time to reach out to its immediate community. A young, energetic couple agreed to lead an outreach to the neighborhood children. The couple planned a block party in the neighborhood park to kick off the outreach plan. At the successful block party, the children were invited to attend Vacation Bible School at the church.

A large group of children attended the Vacation Bible School. During the week, they sang and learned about Christ. They prayed. They heard Bible stories. But they also ran in the hallways. They were loud. They spilled drinks on the floors. They opened doors they shouldn't have opened. In short, the church had rules and the new neighborhood kids broke most of them. The congregation could not imagine ministry that included un-churched kids behaving like... un-churched kids! Could God work in the middle of such chaos?

On Sunday, an impromptu meeting was held and a list of the violations and concerns was aired. One person noted that the carpet in the church was fairly new and would not fare well with all of the kids' traffic and spills. Someone proposed that the outreach be discontinued. The church agreed.

In the end, the rules would be enforced. The church people were happy. The disappointed young couple left the church. The neighborhood children had one less opportunity to learn about Christ. The unwitting message that the church shouted to its community was: *we value rules over people.*

LUKE 13:10–17

[10] On a Sabbath Jesus was teaching in one of the synagogues, [11] and a woman was there who had been crippled by a spirit for eighteen years. She was bent over and could not straighten up at all. [12] When Jesus saw her, he called her forward and said to her, "Woman, you are set free from your infirmity." [13] Then he put his hands on her, and immediately she straightened up and praised God. [14] Indignant because Jesus had healed on the Sabbath, the synagogue ruler said to the people, "There are six days for work. So come and be healed on those days, not on the Sabbath." [15] The Lord answered him, "You hypocrites! Doesn't each of you on the Sabbath untie his ox or donkey from the stall and lead it out to give it water? [16] Then should not this woman, a daughter of Abraham, whom Satan has kept bound for eighteen long years, be set free on the Sabbath day from what bound her?" [17] When he said this, all his opponents were humiliated, but the people were delighted with all the wonderful things he was doing.

Called to Revolutionary Compassion (13:10–13)

No one would have been surprised to find Jesus at a synagogue on the Sabbath. Jesus' presence that day was expected. It was the custom of the day for a male Jew. In fact, it was more than just a custom. It was the rule.

What about teaching on the Sabbath? That was status quo for a rabbi. It was expected. It was almost a rule. As Luke begins to set the stage for this story of a day in the life of Jesus, we find nothing out of place. There's nothing unusual about this scene. Yet.

What Jesus would do next would be the talk of the town for months to come. His action would be so counter-cultural it would evoke the ire of the religious establishment even as it drew the awe of the community. Yet the act would be so simple that he would expect his followers to do exactly the same. What was this revolutionary act? Jesus saw a need and he moved to meet it.

What did Jesus see? Jesus saw a woman who had suffered with a crippling infirmity for eighteen years. The author, Luke the physician, is careful to diagnose the source of the woman's infirmity. A "spirit" was responsible for the eighteen year crippling the woman had suffered (Luke 13:11). There was evidence the "spirit" was brought about by the agent of darkness. Jesus declared the woman had been "kept bound" by Satan himself (Luke 13:16).

The woman's life had been overwhelmed by this disease. Unable to stand up straight, she was condemned to live her life hunched over. She had to eat, perform household chores, interact with her neighbors, and sleep in this wretched posture. Every act of every day was a reminder of her crippling infirmity and her need for healing.

What is the most devastating need you have ever encountered? Was the sight so overwhelming that it paralyzed you? Did it move you to tears? Did it move you at all? More importantly, did you move?

Jesus' initiative in healing the woman is telling. "When Jesus saw her, he called her" (Luke 13:12). He did not wait to see if the woman would call out to him. Jesus would not be a reactionary force waiting to be unleashed only when the woman chose to take the first step. Jesus would initiate her healing.

God is often described in Scripture as the initiator. "For God so loved the world that he gave his one and only son" (John 3:16a). The Creator did not wait for a response to his love. He did not condition the giving of his Son on whether his love would be received or returned. His love for the world moved him to give.

God decided that it was not enough to just profess his love for us. He chose to show us his powerful love. "God demonstrates his own love for us in this: While we were still sinners, Christ died for us" (Romans 5:8). God shows us that revolutionary compassion requires initiative.

Revolutionary compassion also requires intentional interaction. Luke described Jesus' progressive interaction with the woman in need. First, Jesus "saw her." Then he "called her." Jesus then spoke to her. And finally, he "put his hands on her" (Luke 13:12–13).

Each progressive interaction was more involved. With each step taken, the woman was closer to having her need met. Each step taken could have easily been the last step taken. Jesus could have seen the woman, and stopped there. He could have called to her and then done nothing. After his conversation with the woman, Jesus could have determined there was no use in doing more. Choosing to take the next revolutionary, compassionate step, Jesus touched her and healed her.

Have you ever stopped too soon? Have you seen a need and decided it was not your concern? Did you take a few steps, examine the need a little closer, and decide to stop and do nothing? Right now you could be one step away from bringing revolutionary compassion to someone who desperately needs it. Don't stop now. Take the next step. Meet the need in Jesus' name.

Religious Rules Inhibit the Work of Healing (13:14)

After eighteen years of suffering, the woman's healing came in an instant! You might expect a chorus of "Hallelujah's" intermixed with ecstatic "Amen's" to rise from the crowd. Surely the religious leaders would be at the forefront of celebrating this miraculous move of

God. The glorious work happened in their very presence. Undoubtedly their hearts would swell with holy awe. This was not the case.

To the contrary, the synagogue leader was indignant. Jesus' act of healing did not fit into his pre-existing religious template. The religious leader had never considered the possibility of the God of the Sabbath choosing to reveal his glory in this way, and on this day. You can imagine the religious analysis going on in his head: *Take one miraculous work—check. Execute it in the synagogue—check. Experience a miracle—check. Perform it on a Sabbath— wait just a minute!*

Jesus' act of meeting the woman's need for healing broke the mold of the religious leader's experience. According to the leader's rule book, God did not work that way. He could only draw one conclusion and admonished the crowd with it: "There are six days for work. So come and be healed on those days, not on the Sabbath" (Luke 13:14).

Interestingly enough, the ruler did not deny the miraculous work of Christ. He did not even want to prevent it or reverse it. He just wanted the people around him to come back and experience their healing at a time that fit into his religious schedule.

Take a look at your religious rule book. What restrictions have you placed on when God is able to work? Have you restricted him to work only on Sundays and Wednesdays? What are your boundaries for where God can reveal his glory? Must he do it at church, during a

Bible study, or in other "spiritual" environments? How about on a baseball field, at the grocery store or in a restaurant? What will you choose to do when God works outside of your religious rubric?

You must determine now what you will do when God works outside of your template. You must choose to accept that God wants to help others. He wants to do it through you. And he will do it when, where, and how he chooses to do so—even when it makes us uncomfortable. Choose today not to add restrictions to the healing work God wants to do in you and through you.

Religious Rules Cripple the Work of Freedom (13:15–17)

Jesus' response was swift and unequivocal, "You hypocrites!" (Luke 13:15). Note that the text reflects *one* synagogue leader expressed his disapproval of the Sabbath miracle. But, Jesus responds in the *plural*—"hypocrites." He knew, in addition to the leader, there were others who disapproved of his work. It appears the practice of valuing procedure over people can be contagious. Others will be influenced by the way we respond when God chooses to work outside of our predetermined patterns.

Jesus reminded them of one of their own Sabbath practices. They untied their animals from their stalls in order to lead them to drink. It was a Sabbath act of compassion to care for the animals. The unleashing was both *from* something and *for* something. It was a liberating act of freedom.

If such an act was permissible in their rulebook for animals, why not for a "daughter of Abraham"(13:16)? By describing the woman in this way, Jesus was tying her identity to the religious leaders' most respected spiritual icon—Abraham. As a daughter of Abraham, she was their sister in the faith, and the liberating work of Jesus in her life was to be valued. Jesus clearly pointed out the religious leaders had grown to love fundamentalist formulas over freedom.

Jesus' healing work and subsequent teaching on it produced two stark and contradictory responses from those who observed his miracle. The religious leaders who opposed him were humiliated. But the people "were delighted with all the wonderful things he was doing" (13:17).

How is it that the same liberating act of compassion, produced by the same divine power, could produce such distinct reactions? The answer is the value system through which the miracle was experienced. One group valued religious principles over people. When their expectations were not met, nothing else mattered. Not healing. Not freedom. Not a miracle.

The other group chose to simply delight in the wonder of Jesus' work—whenever and however he chose to do it. How will you respond?

Applying This Truth to My Life

Jesus initiated a revolutionary act of compassion. He incrementally approached the woman until her need was met. In doing so, Jesus acted outside the scope of the preconceived notions the religious leaders had about faith. Jesus chose to value the woman and her healing over the reluctance of the rest. Jesus engaged the spiritual leaders and challenged them to re-examine their templates of faith. Today he challenges you to re-evaluate your preconceived notions of faith and ministry. Jesus chose to value people over rules. Will you?

SABBATH RULES

It was a simple command— "Remember the Sabbath day by keeping it holy" (Exodus 20:8). But people wondered, *how do we do it?* The challenge began when people attempted to put the simple command into practice. Teachings and practices were examined, re-examined, and amplified. Corollaries or related rules began to be written. For example, everyone agreed the Sabbath was a day of rest—no work should be performed. But what is work? To answer the question, *work rules* were developed. Eventually the *work rules* had developed into thirty-nine categories of "melakha" (work). These restrictions included the prohibition of boiling water or toasting bread. You were not to make any of the following perform work functions on the Sabbath: your children, employees, or any animals you owned. Lighting a fire was also considered work. Some modern day observers of the fire-lighting prohibition will not light a match or a gas stove. Nor will they add firewood to a fire. Other extensions of the rule prohibit turning electricity on or off; especially if it turns on a furnace, or moving a thermostat's temperature control.

UNUSUAL TEACHING METHODS

Cathy, the Children's Minister, loves the kids at church. She is very creative in her teaching strategies. Your daughter impresses you by reciting a Bible verse and a powerful biblical principle that she learned in Cathy's class. Unfortunately, your excitement quickly wanes when you discover that Cathy is using some unusual teaching methods. Her practices aren't sinful or destructive. You don't deny their effectiveness with the children. Still, Cathy's methods lie outside your previous educational experience. How do you resolve your discomfort with Cathy's teaching methods in a way that ensures the children's learning needs are being met?

QUESTIONS

1. What was your response the last time that someone broke a rule in front of you?

2. Can you remember a time when someone took the initiative to help you? How did you feel?

3. What are some of the things that keep us from taking the next step in meeting someone's need?

4. What are some rules regarding church, ministry, or faith that are not in the Bible but are in your own rulebook?

5. Which of your religious rules would be the hardest to break? What result would be worth breaking your rule?

UNIT TWO

Making a Personal Choice

Unit two, "Making a Personal Choice" is comprised of four lessons from Luke 14–19 that present challenging questions for those who choose to follow Christ. Lesson six focuses on the cost of discipleship while lesson seven warns about the danger of spiritual pride. Lesson eight challenges disciples in the area of their priorities and lesson nine calls us to evaluate our response to the personal invitation of Jesus.

UNIT TWO: MAKING A PERSONAL CHOICE

Lesson 6	Sacrifice or Security?	Luke 14:25–35
Lesson 7	Pride or Humility?	Luke 18:9–17
Lesson 8	Riches or Relationship?	Luke 18:18–30
Lesson 9	Repentance or Rebuke?	Luke 19:1–10

FOCAL TEXT
Luke 14:25–35

BACKGROUND
Luke 9:23–27,
57–62; 14:25–35

LESSON SIX
Sacrifice or Security?

MAIN IDEA

One should carefully consider the personal sacrifice required to be a disciple of Jesus.

QUESTION TO EXPLORE

What are the costs associated with being a disciple of Jesus?

STUDY AIM

To define the costs associated with being a disciple of Jesus, and to evaluate my willingness to follow him through sacrificial obedience

QUICK READ

Jesus used three illustrations to challenge the crowds to determine whether or not they would be willing to follow him, no matter what it would cost them.

Not too long ago, my husband and I decided to add a sun-room to our home. We asked several contractors to bid on the cost of the addition. We costed out several options—full-length windows, additional air ducts, electrical outlets, types of wood, insulation, roofing, and siding. Based on the bids, we decided what we were able to do given our budget and our needs. We never would have asked a builder to start construction without first knowing the cost.

In much the same way, Jesus challenged his followers to calculate the cost of following him. Today's focal passage shows that being a disciple of Jesus is not simply a matter of intellectual assent or following a behavioral creed. Following Jesus means surrendering your life to him.

LUKE 14:25–35

25 Large crowds were traveling with Jesus, and turning to them he said: **26** "If anyone comes to me and does not hate his father and mother, his wife and children, his brothers and sisters—yes, even his own life—he cannot be my disciple. **27** And anyone who does not carry his cross and follow me cannot be my disciple. **28** "Suppose one of you wants to build a tower. Will he not first sit down and estimate the cost to see if he has enough money to complete it? **29** For if he lays the foundation and is not able to finish it, everyone who sees it will ridicule him, **30** saying, 'This fellow began to build and was not able to finish.' **31** "Or suppose a king is about to go to war against another king. Will he not first sit down and consider whether he is able with ten thousand men to oppose the one coming against him with twenty thousand? **32** If he is not able, he will send a delegation while the other is still a long way off and will ask for terms of peace. **33** In the same way, any of you who does not give up everything he has cannot be my disciple. **34** "Salt is good, but if it loses its saltiness, how can it be made salty again? **35** It is fit neither for the soil nor for the manure pile; it is thrown out. "He who has ears to hear, let him hear."

Who Do You Hate? (14:25–27)

This was not the first time the crowds heard Jesus talk about the sacrifice involved in being a disciple (follower) of Jesus. A few chapters earlier, in Luke 9:23–27, Jesus talked about losing one's life in order to save it. He challenged the people to avoid striving to gain everything and lose their souls in the process. Later in that chapter (9:57–62), Jesus refuted the excuses people gave about following him. In doing so, he was making a point: I am more important than anything else in your life.

The focal passage for today (Luke 14:25–35) took place just after Jesus told a parable about the kingdom of God.

In that parable, the master of the home invites "the poor, the crippled, the blind, and the lame" to a grand banquet (14:21). No doubt, the crowd would have made the connection to their own lives. Jesus was inviting them to be a part of the kingdom of God. Jesus' open and graceful acceptance of the marginalized and ordinary person made him very popular. Hence, large crowds followed him on his way to Jerusalem. They thought he would be the Messiah who would overthrow the government and establish God's kingdom on earth. Despite the throngs, however, Jesus wasn't interested in a mob following driven by popularity. He wanted true disciples.

Jesus used the word "hate" to describe one's affection toward other people in comparison to one's love for Jesus (14:26). Clearly, Jesus was not telling the crowds to hate people, because that mentality is completely contrary to his mission of love and mercy. He was not telling children to hate their parents or husbands to mistreat their wives. Rather, Jesus was using hyperbole, exaggerating his point to show what true discipleship should look like. Nothing should come between you and God—not even the people whom you love the most. Love for Christ should be greater than love for family. In fact, a person's walk with Christ may come at the cost of those relationships.

Early Christians experienced the results of such sacrifice. Many of their family members were killed, their homes taken away, and their livelihoods destroyed because of their faith in Jesus. Many of them, including most of the disciples, were killed because they chose to follow Jesus. While that kind of sacrifice seems far removed from today's American culture, believers in other countries know firsthand the cost of following him. In countries like Nigeria, Somalia, Algeria, and Pakistan, being a devout disciple of Jesus could mean severe discrimination, persecution, confiscation of property, imprisonment, and even death.

Jesus took the analogy even further and made it more personal by demanding that his followers carry their own cross (14:27). The people to whom Jesus was speaking clearly understood that carrying one's cross was a walk to death. In making this bold statement, Jesus was helping the crowds understand that following him meant more than merely agreeing with his teachings. It meant surrendering one's life to him, no matter the outcome.

In today's culture, such a commitment to Jesus is not popular. People would rather hear about all that Jesus can do for them instead of hearing about the cost of following him. It's easier to sit comfortably in the pew than to sacrifice one's time, money, hobbies, or relationships in obedience to God's calling. That kind of message is rarely embraced by the mainstream culture.

What Will It Cost You? (14:28–33)

To illustrate the need to choose wisely about following him, Jesus used two analogies that the people readily understood. First, he talked about building a tower. No one would start building a structure without first calculating how much it would cost. Otherwise, the builder might run out of money before the building was complete. The result would be wasted time and wasted money.

In the second illustration, Jesus told about a king who calculated the cost of going to war. No king who cared about his troops or his own life would run ahead into battle without first knowing what he was up against. Instead, a wise king would evaluate whether or not he had the troops and armaments capable of winning the battle. If not, he would find a diplomatic solution. There was no sense in going to battle when defeat would be both certain and costly.

In much the same way, a person must seriously consider whether or not he is willing to "give up everything" (14:32) to be a disciple of Jesus. In both parables, moving ahead hastily could be just as costly as going forward without evaluating the situation critically, showing the need to count the cost. Unfortunately, many people rush headlong into following Jesus without first thinking about whether or not they are "all in." Faced with struggle or difficulty, many of these people become angry and bitter at God for the trouble they are facing because they didn't "sign up for this." They want the assurance of heaven and the promise of blessings, but are unwilling to endure the hardship of following Christ. In the end, they become defeated, discouraged, and sidelined from their journey of faith. Their haste costs them dearly.

What is implied, but not stated, is that both the builder and the king had to evaluate both sides of the scenario. What are the drawbacks if I don't build? What might it cost me if I don't go to battle? While many people turn away because they understand the costs of following Jesus, they fail to take into consideration what it will cost them if they don't follow Jesus. While following Jesus involves sacrifice, the rewards of following Jesus far outweigh any negative consequences. Not only does an unbeliever face an eternity in hell without Christ, he or she also faces a life lacking in hope, peace, and purpose. Such a person misses out on the joy of a relationship with Jesus, the unique fellowship shared among believers, and the abiding presence of the Spirit of God who sustains and supports a person through the most painful and dark moments of life.

Losing Your Flavor (14:34–35)

Jesus' closing statements in this chapter may seem a bit out of place. One minute he is talking about builders and kings, and the next minute, he's talking about salt. What does salt and saltiness have to do with counting the cost of following Jesus?

Jesus was using another illustration to challenge his disciples against halfhearted, lukewarm discipleship. In biblical times, salt served two main functions. First, it was used as a preservative for meats. Because there was no refrigeration at that time, meat was cooked immediately and then salted to be eaten later. Second, salt would be used as a flavoring, hence Jesus talked about saltiness.

The salt in New Testament times was taken from water in the area, most prominently the Dead Sea. It was not pure and was often mixed with other minerals and elements in the water. It could become so contaminated by these other elements that it was no longer usable for either preservation or flavor. It could not even be placed on the manure pile. If mixed with manure, the manure could not be used as fertilizer because the salt would kill the vegetation.

The point? As "salt of the earth" (Matt. 5:13), disciples who become contaminated by the world—by their own agendas and their own sin—lose their saltiness. Unsalty salt—lukewarm believers—no longer serve a useful function. They are useless to the kingdom because their flavor, once unique and appealing, no longer attracts people to Jesus. This was another challenge for prospective disciples to consider before choosing to follow him.

Implications and Actions

Very soon after this encounter, the disciples would count the cost of following Jesus themselves. While they all deserted him at the crucifixion, they all returned (with the exception of Judas) to follow him at great peril and enormous personal cost. Perhaps their time away from the Savior taught them an important lesson: the cost of being without Jesus is too great. Following him is worth it all, even today. The question for every person to answer is this: Are you willing to follow him, no matter what?

DISCIPLE

Used often in the Gospels, the term "disciple" as used in biblical times referred to any student, apprentice, or follower of someone's teaching. Such disciples submitted themselves to the teacher, spent time with the teacher, and learned as much as possible as apprentices. The term "disciple" was used in conjunction with philosophers (such as Plato or Socrates), teachers of crafts (such as art or carpentry), or political leaders of the day. It eventually became a term most often used to refer to pupils who followed a particular religious leader. For example, John the Baptist had a group of followers who were dedicated to his teachings. So did many other popular rabbis.

APPLYING THE SCRIPTURE

To apply this story in your daily life:

- Ask yourself, "What things are coming between me and my relationship with Jesus?"

- Rid your life of those things that contaminate your saltiness as a disciple

- Write down how following Jesus has cost you

- Write down how following Jesus has changed you, your family, and your friends

- This week, ask Jesus to give you the opportunity to be salt in another person's life, whetting their appetite for a relationship with him.

QUESTIONS

1. Thinking back on your own conversion (decision to follow Jesus), did you evaluate the costs of following him? Why or why not?

2. How has following Jesus been costly for someone you know?

3. What has following Jesus cost you? Your family?

4. What would *not* following Jesus cost you? Your family?

5. How have you lost your "saltiness" in your sphere of influence?

LESSON SEVEN
Pride or Humility?

MAIN IDEA

Jesus used the Parable of the Pharisee and the Tax Collector to illustrate our need to approach God with an attitude of humble dependence.

QUESTION TO EXPLORE

What is the typical attitude of your heart as you approach God in prayer?

STUDY AIM

To examine my heart for any evidence of pride and to humbly repent if any is found

QUICK READ

Jesus highlighted two different approaches to God in prayer: a Pharisee who focused on himself, and a tax collector who was humble in the presence of God.

In today's culture of self-promotion, it's hard to develop an attitude of humility. It's easy to get caught up in how many friends you have on Facebook, how many Twitter followers you've gained, how many people follow your blog, or how many people look at your Pinterest boards. Over time, such popularity can be intoxicating. This lesson shows the result of living for the applause of others and demanding the applause of God, too.

LUKE 18:9–17

9 To some who were confident of their own righteousness and looked down on everybody else, Jesus told this parable: 10 "Two men went up to the temple to pray, one a Pharisee and the other a tax collector. 11 The Pharisee stood up and prayed about himself: 'God, I thank you that I am not like other men—robbers, evildoers, adulterers—or even like this tax collector. 12 I fast twice a week and give a tenth of all I get.' 13 "But the tax collector stood at a distance. He would not even look up to heaven, but beat his breast and said, 'God, have mercy on me, a sinner.' 14 "I tell you that this man, rather than the other, went home justified before God. For everyone who exalts himself will be humbled, and he who humbles himself will be exalted." 15 People were also bringing babies to Jesus to have him touch them. When the disciples saw this, they rebuked them. 16 But Jesus called the children to him

and said, "Let the little children come to me, and do not hinder them, for the kingdom of God belongs to such as these. **17** I tell you the truth, anyone who will not receive the kingdom of God like a little child will never enter it."

Two Men, Two Examples (18:9–10)

Many times in the Gospels, the writer does not provide a reason for Jesus' actions. However, in this story, Luke explains exactly why Jesus told this particular parable: "To some who were confident of their own righteousness and looked down on everyone else" (Luke 18:9). As he did throughout his ministry, Jesus confronted the self-righteous attitude found among many of the Jews of that day. As God's people, they were supposed to be a light to other nations, but they had become smug as God's chosen people. The worst among the self-righteous were the religious leaders of the day. Jesus confronted their hypocritical attitudes and actions on more than one occasion (see Matt. 23:1–36; Luke 11:37–44).

On this occasion, Jesus compared a Pharisee to a tax collector. In that day, there would have been no greater polar opposites than these two in Jewish culture. The Pharisees were a religious sect within Judaism. They adhered strictly to the law of Moses and other sections of the Old Testament (as we know it today) and focused on ceremonial regulations and purity. While their motives may have been pure at one time, their devotion to the letter of the law blinded them to the reasons for the law.

On the other end of the religious and moral spectrum was the tax collector. He was hated among his fellow Jews because he collected taxes for the Roman government, who ruled over the Jewish people with an iron fist. Most tax collectors would become rich by inflating the taxes and pocketing the profits, becoming wealthy at the expense of fellow Jews. After encountering Jesus, one such tax collector, Zachaeus, promised to repay those whom he had cheated (Luke 19:2–10). Seeing a Pharisee at the temple would have been an ordinary occurrence, but seeing a tax collector would have been unexpected.

Both men "went up to the temple" (18:10). This is in reference to the location of the temple, which stood upon a hill. When they arrived, both men stood to pray, which was the common posture of prayer for the Jewish people. This is where the similarities between the two men end. Once at the temple, the two couldn't be more different in their attitudes and their actions.

One Talks to Himself (18:11–12)

Jesus described the Pharisee first. He said that the Pharisee "stood up and prayed about himself" (18:11). Instead of addressing God in reverence and awe, the

Pharisee addressed the crowd. He spouted off a litany of his accomplishments as a means of self-glorification and a hammer of judgment to others. In doing so, he repeated the word "I" four times. The Pharisee might have been speaking words at God, but he was actually praying to himself because his focus was on himself, not God. His desire was to show off his self-righteousness, not to align his heart with God's.

He first thanked God for what he was not—a robber, an evildoer, an adulterer, or even a tax collector. Clearly this was a statement of judgment toward those around him who were less holy and devoted than he was. He reminded God of all of the things that he didn't do and then reminded God of all of the good things he did do. It is important to notice that in both lists, the focus was on outward behavior, not inward attitude.

The behaviors the Pharisee listed in his prayer reflected an adherence to God's law and Jewish tradition. He fasted twice a week as many other Jews did. They fasted on the fifth day of the week, in reverence for the day that Moses went up on Mount Sinai to receive the law. They also fasted on the second day of the week to commemorate the day that Moses came down from Mount Sinai. In addition, he gave a tenth of everything he had, not just what the Old Testament required. The Pharisee went above and beyond the minimal requirements of the law that the average Jew would follow. Clearly he believed that strict adherence to the law made him holy and whole before God. He was depending on his own power and good deeds. Nowhere in his soliloquy did the Pharisee ask God for anything. Paul would later condemn such pride in keeping the law (Rom. 3:27).

It's hard to picture how anyone could be so proud and arrogant before God, but believers today are just as guilty as the Pharisee. It is just carefully covered up with spiritual terminology. Gossip about others' failures becomes prayer requests and believers silently thank God for not being caught up in those sins—adultery, homosexuality, tax evasion, or the like.

One Talks to God (18:13)

In sharp contrast to the Pharisee, the tax collector "stood at a distance," (Luke 18:13) which indicates that he was not concerned with having the spotlight. Rather than fix his eyes upward as was customary for Jews, he would not look up because of his shame and the awareness of his sin. Instead, he beat his chest. The verb "beat" carries the idea of continual action. He kept on beating his chest in self-reproach and in grief over his sin. Clearly, the tax collector understood his state before God.

His prayer to God was simple: "God, have mercy on me, a sinner" (18:13). The tax collector used seven words to throw himself at the mercy seat of God, a stark contrast to the Pharisee whose rambling monologue was thirty-three words in length. The emphasis of the tax collector's prayer was different. The focus was clearly on God and his gracious mercy, not on some litany of religious activities that could be checked off as accomplished. The tax collector showed that no flowery words were necessary. What mattered was a heart humbled by the recognition of one's sinful state before a holy and righteous God. Perhaps the most heartfelt prayers are simple: God have mercy, God help me. Thank you, God.

In every church that meets together for worship and prayer, a mixture of people will gather in the congregation. Some are like the Pharisee, so self-absorbed and so proud of their own accomplishments that they are completely blind to their sin and need for rescue. They rely on their good deeds, their financial security, or even their status in the community to provide spiritual security. Some are like the tax collector, very aware of their great need before God. In reality, any of us could play the role of the Pharisee. This happens when we forget the grace and mercy of the God who has saved us and when we judge others in the congregation who are "worse" sinners. When our thoughts are occupied with wondering whether or not we look good on the outside and are afraid of others' knowing what's inside, we too have become self-absorbed.

A Blessing and a Warning (18:14)

Jesus must have shocked the crowds when he pronounced the tax collector as justified rather than the Pharisee. First, he proclaimed someone righteous, which was something that only God could do. In doing so, he was equating himself with God. Secondly, he proclaimed the wrong person as justified. Surely the Pharisee deserved God's favor instead of the tax collector. After all, he had followed the law with precise obedience. Third, Jesus announced that the tax collector had been justified—immediately. The word justified meant more than forgiveness. It also included being declared not guilty. No additional sacrifice or acts of penance were necessary.

Notice the statement Jesus made at the end of the parable: "For everyone who exalts himself will be humbled, and he who humbles himself will be exalted" (18:14b). This statement turned the religious norms upside down. Instead of being exalted, the self-righteous and prideful person would be brought down while God would honor the humble. The reason for the tax collector's justification was directly tied to his approach of humility toward God; it had absolutely nothing to do with his good deeds. The tax collector saw himself clearly—that he wasn't self-sufficient or self-righteous. He saw himself as a sinner in need of God's mercy. God will not turn away the person who humbly approaches him.

Living Example: Be Childlike (18:15–17)

After this parable, the people brought infants and children to Jesus. Although the crowds understood humility because they saw it in Jesus, apparently the disciples still struggled with the trait because the disciples thought that children weren't worth their time. Jesus used this opportunity to further illustrate what true humility looks like. First, he paid attention to a group of people—children—who were considered unimportant. Second, Jesus put his hands on the children, blessing them. He didn't consider himself too good to spend time with children. Kids can be messy and stinky and demanding, but that didn't matter to him. Scripture says, "Jesus called the children to him" (18:16). He invited the least of these (Matt. 19:13) to himself.

Jesus said that the kingdom of God belonged to "such as these" (Luke 18:16). He was not saying that only children would enter God's kingdom. Rather, it is the attitude of humility that children possess that is the key to becoming a part of God's family. Children don't care about accolades or checklists used to measure right living. Children don't know how to be fake and pretentious. They don't bring their resumé of religious activity to God for his approval. They simply come to God with faith and trust. The rest doesn't matter. That is the mark of true humility.

Implications and Actions

In today's culture of self-grandiosity and self-promotion, this parable stands out in sharp contrast to the way many people live, even in Christian circles. The point of Jesus' story is clear: outward acts are useless if they do not flow from a heart of humility toward God and others. It is a challenging reminder.

PHARISEE

The Pharisees were a group of men within Judaism who held to a strict set of beliefs. They were committed to the written law, (specifically the Pentateuch, or the first five books of the Bible), as well as the oral law, which was comprised of the traditional teachings of the rabbis handed down throughout many generations. Over time, the Pharisees asserted that this oral law had been given to Moses by God himself and was just as authoritative as the written Scriptures. This adherence to traditions and rules was at the heart of the conflict between the Pharisees and Jesus. For example, when the disciples ate with unclean hands (which was an oral tradition, not a biblical command), the Pharisees confronted Jesus. In that confrontation, Jesus challenged the Pharisees' adherence to tradition while simultaneously ignoring God's commands (Mark 7:1–8ff).

HUMILITY CHECK

This week, as you reflect on Christ's call to humility, grade yourself in the following areas (on a scale of A-F). Then, ask God to develop humility where needed.

_____Humility toward coworkers

_____Humility toward your children

_____Humility toward your spouse

_____Humility toward fellow church members

_____Humility toward friends

_____Humility toward the poor

QUESTIONS

1. How are you sometimes like the Pharisee? How are you sometimes like the tax collector?

2. How do you know when pride is creeping into your relationship with God?

3. What is the difference between humility and self-deprecation?

4. What qualities of children's faith do you want in your own life?

LESSON EIGHT

Riches or Relationship?

MAIN IDEA

A rich ruler placed greater value on his material wealth than on his relationship with God.

QUESTION TO EXPLORE

What competing priorities keep us from being fully devoted followers of Jesus?

STUDY AIM

To honestly evaluate the things in my life that take priority over my relationship with Jesus

QUICK READ

Jesus met a rich man who wanted to know how to earn eternal life. Jesus used this encounter to teach the importance of seeking God above all else.

The one with the most toys wins.

Perhaps you've seen that phrase on a bumper sticker or as a t-shirt logo. This attitude toward money and possessions is common in today's opulent culture of materialism. This attitude was also at the heart of Jesus' discussion with the rich young ruler. Jesus challenged the man to leave behind what he loved the most—his money—and to follow him instead. Jesus knew something that the rich man didn't: the one with the most toys needs a Savior.

LUKE 18:18–30

18 A certain ruler asked him, "Good teacher, what must I do to inherit eternal life?" **19** "Why do you call me good?" Jesus answered. "No one is good—except God alone. **20** You know the commandments: 'Do not commit adultery, do not murder, do not steal, do not give false testimony, honor your father and mother.'" **21** "All these I have kept since I was a boy," he said. **22** When Jesus heard this, he said to him, "You still lack one thing. Sell everything you have and give to the poor, and you will have treasure in heaven. Then come, follow me." **23** When he heard this, he became very sad, because he was a man of great wealth. **24** Jesus looked at him and said, "How hard it is for the rich to enter the kingdom of God! **25** Indeed, it is easier for a camel to go through the eye of a needle than for a rich man to enter the kingdom of God." **26** Those who heard this asked, "Who then can be saved?" **27** Jesus replied, "What is impossible with men is possible with God." **28** Peter said to him, "We have left all we had to follow you!" **29** "I tell you the truth," Jesus said to them, "no one who has left home or wife or brothers or parents or children for the sake of the kingdom of God **30** will fail to receive many times as much in this age and, in the age to come, eternal life."

A Man, His Question, and Jesus' Answer (18:18–21)

A ruler came up to Jesus and asked him a question. What the man ruled is uncertain, but the term is probably used to highlight the man's wealth (Luke 18:23). He was probably a religious or civic leader. The Gospel of Mark indicates that this man ran up to Jesus and knelt before him (Mark 10:17), which was a symbol of humility. He addressed Jesus with the term "Good teacher" (Luke 18:18). This was a break from the tradition of that day, because no rabbi was ever given that title, but was rather called rabbi or teacher. The term "good" implied complete goodness and sinlessness. Apparently, this man knew that Jesus was markedly different from the other religious leaders of the day. Jesus would address this term later.

The man asked an important question: "what must I do to inherit eternal life?" (18:18). This question reveals a great deal. First, it confirms that the man was searching for something qualitatively different for his life, something that he had not found even with all of his wealth. Second, the question shows that the rich man saw something unique in Jesus, or else he would not have asked the question in the first place. Something about Jesus appealed to him and his heart's cry for meaning. Third, the man's use of the word "do" implied that he thought he could earn his way to eternal life, assuming it was something he could attain with the right effort.

While this question was asked centuries ago, people are still asking themselves the same question: how can I find meaning in my life? What does it mean to find life? And people spend their entire lives in the search for an answer to that question. Some turn to wealth and the acquisition of possessions, thinking that an abundance of stuff can bring fulfillment. Others pursue a career or the next rung on the corporate ladder, thinking the applause of colleagues and supervisors will bring satisfaction. People cling to a myriad of things—drugs, other people, food, pleasure, a smaller waistline, even religion—all in an attempt to find life. Like this rich man, many people never learn an important truth: eternal life cannot be obtained outside of a relationship with God through Christ.

In response to the man, Jesus answered his question with a question, which was a common practice among rabbis. He asked the man, "Why do you call me good?" (18:19). He went on to say, "No one is good—except God alone" (18:19b). Notice that Jesus was not denying his goodness and did not deny that he was God. Rather, he was challenging the ruler to think about why he was calling Jesus "good." This was meant to help the man evaluate his beliefs about Jesus. What is it about me that you seek? Why are you asking me?

After addressing the man's motives, Jesus answered his question by pointing him to the Old Testament law. As a ruler, this man would have been educated, and would have known the commandments. Jesus specifically quoted the second half of the Ten Commandments found in Exodus 20:12–16, which would have been considered easier to keep. The man indicated that he'd kept all of those laws. Would this have been possible? Perhaps, depending on the man's interpretation of the requirements found in the commandments. However, while he might have kept the letter of the law, the rich man most likely failed at the heart level. He might not have murdered anyone, but he may have well harbored anger (see Matt. 5:21–22).

Losing Nothing, Losing Everything (18:22–23)

Notice that the conversation did not end there. The man did not walk away content with Jesus' initial answer. Obviously the man knew there was more to eternal life than keeping the Ten Commandments; or else he would have been content in his current condition or could have talked to the rabbis about his quandary. Instead, he was

waiting for Jesus to comment further, like a pupil waiting for a teacher. He knew something was still missing.
His silence was like saying, Ok. Got that. What else do I
need to do? In that silence, Jesus looked at him and loved
him (Mark 10:21). Obviously, Jesus was peering into the
man's heart and not focusing on his outward appearance.
Jesus knew the one thing that was getting in the way of
the man's allegiance to God.

Jesus' response cut to the heart of the issue. He said,
"You still lack one thing: sell everything you have . . . Then
come, follow me" (Luke 18:22). It's interesting that Jesus
told a rich man that he was lacking something, since rich
people lack nothing materially. The man would not have
missed this play on words. Nor did the man miss the significance of the command. Jesus had cut through the surface
religious adherence to law and went straight for the idol in
the man's heart: his wealth. It was the one thing that occupied the central place in the man's life, and it was the one
thing he was unwilling to let go of. The man's riches were
the chains that bound him. He had everything—prestige,
money, religious piety—and yet he was in bondage.

Jesus challenged the rich man in regard to his following
of the first half of the Old Testament law, the command to
"Love the Lord your God with all your heart and with all
your soul and with all your strength" (Deut. 6:5). The man
did not love God more than anything else. His wealth got
in the way, even though Jesus promised him treasure in
heaven. The things of this life meant more.

Mark's account says, "At this the man's face fell. He went away sad, because he had great wealth" (Mark 10:22). Jesus wasn't purposely trying to make the rich man sad. Rather, Jesus was trying to point out the one thing that would provide lasting joy—following him—but the man was unwilling to follow Jesus' command. And he walked away. This is the only occurrence of someone in the Gospels refusing a direct invitation from Jesus to discipleship. The others, like the disciples, left their old lives behind to follow him.

The man was not the only one who was sad that day. Jesus must have been grieved in his heart that the rich man made the choice to love money rather than to follow him. The man had everything but was still empty. Yet, Jesus will not force anyone to follow him, so he allowed the rich man to walk away. Watching a loved child rebel must have pierced the Father's heart as well.

Camels, Needles, and Impossibilities (18:24–27)

After watching the man walk away sad, Jesus made a statement that must have confounded the disciples and others standing around: "How hard it is for the rich to enter the kingdom of God!" (Luke 18:24). In Jesus' day, people erroneously believed that if someone was blessed with wealth, they had God's approval and favor. They thought that the wealthy would surely be in God's kingdom.

To make his point, Jesus used a humorous illustration—a camel going through the eye of a needle. Many people have tried to explain Jesus' reference by claiming that the "eye of a needle" (Luke 18:25) referred to a small, specific gate in Jerusalem that was too small for a camel to pass through. However, most scholars believe Jesus was simply using hyperbole to show the incredible challenge of a rich person entering heaven.

Was Jesus saying that people with wealth cannot enter heaven? No. Early believers like Joseph of Arimathea and Lydia were wealthy. His point was this: wealth and riches are often obstacles to the kingdom of God. Money can lull people into a certain level of satisfaction and blind them to the need for something more than personal pleasure. Living for the moment, such people may believe that nothing exists beyond the here and now, so it's best to live it up and enjoy. They may place their faith in the wealth they have accumulated and fail to recognize their spiritual needs.

Note the question the disciples asked. They were still grappling with the idea that wealth didn't guarantee God's favor. If even the wealthy—those favored by God—couldn't enter the kingdom of God, then what would happen to them, the working class? Jesus reminded them that entering the kingdom of God wasn't a matter of credentials or credit scores or credit card limits. Eternal life comes as a miracle from God as he calls the human heart to a relationship with himself.

Losing Everything, Gaining Everything (18:28–30)

With the promise of treasures in heaven ringing in his ears, Peter asked the question that the rest of the disciples were thinking but were afraid to ask. It was as if Peter were asking, Um, Jesus, we've left everything. What about us? Rather than chastise Peter (which he often had to do), Jesus used Peter's statement as a teachable moment. He assured his followers that they would be blessed beyond measure for their willingness to forsake all and follow him. Obviously, Jesus was not referring to earthly wealth, but rather some sort of spiritual fulfillment or honor. Whatever the treasure is, it is a gift from God, not something to be earned. Eternal life would be the ultimate reward (18:30).

Implications and Actions

The implication is clear: nothing should get in the way of a person's relationship with God. While the rich man struggled with wealth, Christians may struggle with other idols: pride, self-sufficiency, approval of others, legalism, popularity, or even asceticism. Just as the rich young man made a choice, every person must decide whether or not Jesus will be the focus of his or her heart. God will not be relegated to second place. Ask yourself: what competing priorities keep me from being fully devoted to Jesus?

TREASURE

The term treasure or treasury is used throughout the Bible. The original word carried the idea of a casket, coffer, or other storehouse or holding place in which valuables were kept. It also applied to the trumpet-shaped offering holders in the temple court, where Jesus watched people make their offerings. In the Old Testament, a treasure might be stored in the temple (1 Kings 7:51) or in the king's palace (2 Kings 20:13).

In the Old Testament, the term also applied to Israel as God's treasured possession (Ex. 19:5; Deut. 7:6). The writer of Proverbs said that one's memory is a treasured thing (Prov. 2:1; 7:1, NASB), and encouraged the reader to treasure God's commandments (Prov. 7:1, NASB).

The word treasure is also used several times in the New Testament (Matt. 6:21; 13:44; Luke 12:33–34; 2 Cor. 4:7). Mary treasured up the information about her son, Jesus (Luke 2:19). Jesus used the term often, comparing earthly treasures to heavenly ones (Matt. 6:19–20). He also said that what one treasures or values would determine one's actions (Matt. 6:21). Later, Paul used the term to talk about the treasures of wisdom and knowledge found in Christ (Col. 2:3).

EVALUATE

To help evaluate your relationship with God, ask yourself the following questions:

- What would my coworkers and colleagues say is the priority of my life?

- What would my family say is the priority of my life?

- What would my closest friends say is the priority of my life?

- What would my checkbook say is the priority of my life?

If these questions have different answers, consider why the answers differ. If people cannot say that God is the priority of your life, what does that say about you? Ask God to show you the answer to that question.

QUESTIONS

1. Reflecting back on the rich man's actions, what in Jesus' character or demeanor do you think compelled the rich man to seek Jesus out?

2. What kinds of religious actions do people think will earn them a place in the kingdom of God?

3. What things can take priority over a person's relationship with Jesus?

4. What would Jesus say gets in the way of your relationship with him?

LESSON NINE

Repentance or Rebuke?

MAIN IDEA

Zacchaeus, a notorious tax collector, responds to Jesus' personal invitation with repentance and faith.

QUESTION TO EXPLORE

How do we respond to the personal invitation of Jesus?

STUDY AIM

To respond to my personal invitation from Jesus (for salvation and sanctification) with repentance and faith

QUICK READ

Jesus extended his love and offer of discipleship to the most despised of his day—the tax collector. In doing so, Jesus demonstrated his earthly mission.

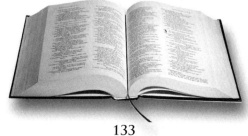

Many of us grew up in Sunday School learning the beloved song about Zacchaeus, the wee little man who climbed up in the sycamore tree because he wanted to see the Lord. Over time, familiarity may breed indifference to this beautiful story of a life changed. Our challenge in today's lesson is to look at it through a new lens—the lens of Zaccheus. Through his eyes, we can see a powerful truth: the Son of Man came to seek and to save the lost. He came to save all of us, from the despised tax collector to the stay-at-home mom, from the most outcast in today's culture to the most accepted. Everyone needs salvation through Jesus, and he is willing to accept anyone who will come to him.

LUKE 19:1–10

[1] Jesus entered Jericho and was passing through. [2] A man was there by the name of Zacchaeus; he was a chief tax collector and was wealthy. [3] He wanted to see who Jesus was, but being a short man he could not, because of the crowd. [4] So he ran ahead and climbed a sycamore-fig tree to see him, since Jesus was coming that way. [5] When Jesus reached the spot, he looked up and said to him, "Zacchaeus, come down immediately. I must stay at your house today." [6] So he came down at once and welcomed him gladly. [7] All the people saw this and began to mutter, "He has gone to be the guest of a 'sinner.'"

8 But Zacchaeus stood up and said to the Lord, "Look, Lord! Here and now I give half of my possessions to the poor, and if I have cheated anybody out of anything, I will pay back four times the amount." **9** Jesus said to him, "Today salvation has come to this house, because this man, too, is a son of Abraham. **10** For the Son of Man came to seek and to save what was lost."

A Man Goes Out on a Limb (19:1–4)

This story takes place in Jericho, which is about seventeen miles east of Jerusalem. Jesus was headed to Jerusalem for the Passion week and his crucifixion. There were many routes Jesus could have traveled to Jerusalem without going through Jericho, which begs the question: Why did Jesus go to Jericho? Why didn't he take a different route? Quite possibly, Jesus knew there was a man there whose heart was yearning for the love and mercy of God. Jesus may have made the detour solely for the purpose of meeting Zacchaeus. This story is only found in this Gospel, and it continues the theme of surprise endings that are often found in Luke.

The name Zacchaeus means "pure" or "innocent," which the man was surely not. He was a "chief tax collector" (Luke 19:2). Tax collectors worked for the Roman Empire, which automatically made them despised by the Jewish people, who longed for freedom from Roman rule. Tax collectors were charged with the task of collecting money for the maintenance of the government. Their salary was derived from charging more than was required by law and then pocketing the profit. Hence, a tax collector was motivated to exact a high tax. A "chief" tax collector would have been on the top of the tax collection hierarchy. Zacchaeus probably contracted with the government to collect the taxes and in turn, hired others to do the actual work. He may have received kickbacks from lower-ranking collectors. Tax collectors were held in the lowest possible esteem for both their occupation (no one likes to pay taxes) and for their greed. They were placed in the same category as prostitutes (Matt. 21:32).

Scripture indicates that Zacchaeus "wanted to see who Jesus was" (Luke 19:3). No doubt, Jesus' arrival was accompanied by much fanfare as the crowds followed and preceded him into the city. Zacchaeus was curious about this visiting celebrity. However, Scripture also reveals that Zacchaeus was short. This created a problem. He could not see over the crowd, and he could not join the crowd because he was hated. Had he tried to work his way through the crowd to get a glimpse of Jesus, he probably would have been mistreated—elbowed, shoved, or even possibly punched or beaten. Undeterred, Zacchaeus enacted Plan B: he ran ahead of the crowd and climbed up a sycamore tree. Both running and climbing a tree would have been undignified for a grown man, especially a wealthy one. No doubt his curiosity outweighed the social stigma. Besides, he was already hated, so he really had nothing to lose.

Jesus Sees and Knows Zacchaeus (19:5–6)

Zacchaeus wanted to catch a glimpse of Jesus, but he got so much more instead. The Bible says that Jesus looked up at Zacchaeus and called him by name (Luke 19:5). This tax collector didn't know who Jesus was, but Jesus knew Zacchaeus—by name. This may have been the first time in many years that Zacchaeus had heard someone say his name in a kind and gentle way. No doubt, Zacchaeus must have been dumbfounded, stunned, and overwhelmed at Jesus' knowing his name and acknowledging his presence.

Not only did Jesus call Zacchaeus by name, he asked to stay in Zacchaeus' house that very day (19:5b). In that day, royalty did not wait for invitations, but rather invited themselves into another's home. This would have been a great honor for the host. The two men would share a meal together. The term "stay" actually carries the idea of staying overnight, so this was more than just a stop in for afternoon tea. In this act, Jesus was reaching out in friendship to a man who was universally despised and rejected. This practice of accepting outcasts was one of the hallmarks of Jesus' actions in the Gospels, it further demonstrated his personal touch.

A Change of Heart (19:7–8)

Jesus' radical request to spend time with Zacchaeus was met with disbelief and disdain by the crowds, who despised sinners like Zacchaeus. It is interesting to note that at the end of the previous chapter, Jesus healed a blind man, after which the people began to praise God. This same crowd began to murmur and complain when similar acts of mercy and grace were bestowed on someone less deserving in their eyes. However, their whining and complaining did not deter Jesus from his mission; nor did it deter Zacchaeus from responding to Jesus' acceptance and friendship.

The evening meal must have taken place between verses seven and eight. In response to his time spent with Jesus, Zacchaeus' heart was moved and changed. He was a transformed man. This was demonstrated by his proclamation to give half of his possessions to the poor and to pay back four-fold anyone he had cheated (19:8). In New Testament times, the law required anyone who had defrauded or cheated another to pay back the amount plus twenty percent. Considering the fact that he had made all of his money by overcharging people on their taxes, the list of people he had cheated must have been quite lengthy. It is interesting to note that nowhere did Jesus demand this show of repentance from Zacchaeus; it was the natural result of a heart transformed by the love of Jesus. While we do not know what took place in the house that evening, we do know that it must have been significant; or else Zacchaeus would have never had such a change of heart.

Zacchaeus' response to Jesus is in sharp contrast to the rich young ruler in the previous chapter (18:18–30). While the young ruler could not give up the idol that was his wealth, Zacchaeus was so changed that money no longer mattered to him. He willingly became a follower of Jesus. In the previous chapter, Jesus indicated that it was very difficult for a rich man to enter heaven, but not impossible. Zacchaeus' transformation is the fulfillment of that truth. Both men faced a choice, but only one had made the right choice.

Insight Into Jesus' Mission (19:9–10)

Jesus' response to Zacchaeus was significant. It was the equivalent of saying, "Welcome to the family!" What a beautiful exchange must have taken place between these two men, one overjoyed at being forgiven and the other overjoyed in offering forgiveness. Jesus called Zacchaeus a "son of Abraham" (19:9). Zacchaeus was already a son of Abraham by birth because he was a Jew. However, as a follower of Jesus, he was now a part of the larger family of God and a participant in God's kingdom. He was welcomed and accepted, not because of his birthright as a Jew, but because of his faith and trust in Jesus. Many Jews were sons of Abraham by birth but never experienced salvation through Jesus.

Luke 19:10 is a summary of the entire book of Luke. Jesus came to earth—and to Jericho that day—to seek and to save the lost. This explanation of his mission is an echo of the parables Jesus spoke in Luke 15 (the parables of the lost sheep, lost coin, and lost son). He demonstrated his mission by seeking out Zacchaeus. Throughout his time on earth, Jesus often extended friendship to notorious sinners like Zacchaeus. Even the worst outcast and most vile offender can find a new beginning in him. All that is required is repentance and placing one's faith and trust in Jesus.

Implications and Actions

Modern readers can find themselves easily in this story. Each person is in need of God's love, mercy, and offer of forgiveness and relationship with Jesus, just like Zacchaeus. And every person must choose whether or not to accept God's offer of relationship. Likewise, anyone can be blinded by his or her own prejudices and pride, like the crowds that day who couldn't understand why Jesus would ever want to spend time with such an outcast. We, too, can be blind to our own sin and need for forgiveness. The question we must all ask, regardless of where we find ourselves in the story, is this: how will I respond to Jesus' offer of forgiveness through a relationship with him?

JERICHO

Jericho is a city mentioned both in the Old Testament and the New Testament. In the Old Testament, it was apparently one of the oldest cities in the world and was the first city that the people of Israel conquered under their leader, Joshua (Josh. 6). According to Genesis 13:10, it was well-watered and favorable for agriculture, just like a garden.

In New Testament times, Jericho was an oasis situated in a hot plain. The combination of rich soil, a constant water source, and the daily sunshine, made it an attractive place to live. In fact, it was much like a resort town because of its lush foliage (hence the sycamore tree), fresh fruits and citrus, natural springs, and fresh water. These attractive elements, combined with the year-round warm climate (nearing eighty degrees in the wintertime), made Jericho a popular vacation spot for the rich. (In fact, Herod the Great built his winter palace there.) It was also known for its groves of balm, which were used medicinally, and for its sycamore trees, which were quite valuable.

It was precisely because of the wealthy who lived there that Zacchaeus probably lived there as well. Taxing the rich who lived in that town would have provided a lucrative income for him, especially being a chief tax collector. When Jesus went to Zacchaeus' home, he probably went to one of the finest and most-prominent homes in the town. This would have been another reason that Zacchaeus was despised by others.

QUESTIONS

1. Who would be the modern-day outcasts and sinners in your church and community? Who would not be welcomed because of their sinful behavior?

2. Reflecting on the story, what do you think happened between Jesus and Zacchaeus during the meal that resulted in such a change in Zacchaeus?

3. What would you willingly give up as a follower of Jesus?

4. Who are you more like in this story—Zacchaeus or the crowd watching this story unfold?

5. Who in your sphere of influence needs to hear that God's grace and forgiveness is available to them, regardless of their sinful actions?

6. How is Jesus inviting you to grow in your relationship with him?

—— U N I T T H R E E ——
Answering Personal Questions

Unit three, "Answering Personal Questions" traces Jesus' responses to various questions from Luke 20–24. His answers speak to his authority (lesson ten), the future (lesson 11), and his identity (lesson twelve.) In lesson thirteen, Jesus uses his encounter on the road to Emmaus to confirm his resurrection and explain the Scriptures to two despondent disciples.

FOCAL TEXT

Luke 20:1–8; 20–26

BACKGROUND

Luke 19:45—20:26

LESSON TEN

Questions about Authority

MAIN IDEA

Jesus responded to deceptive questions on religious and civil authority by pointing to God as the ultimate authority.

QUESTION TO EXPLORE

How can we respond to challenging questions by pointing to God as our ultimate authority?

STUDY AIM

To identify challenging questions I face and to determine to respond to them by pointing to God as my ultimate authority

QUICK READ

When challenged by people who despised his influence, Jesus pointed to God as the ultimate source of authority, not religious or political leaders.

Although not original with him, former U.S. President Harry Truman is credited with popularizing the expression "the buck stops here." These words were on a sign appearing at various times on his desk, a gift from his friend and U.S. Marshal, Fred M. Canfil. Canfil saw a similar sign while visiting a Federal Reformatory in Oklahoma. He knew the practical, plain-speaking president might like it, so he arranged for a copy to be made and sent to Truman.

Derived from the expression "pass the buck," meaning passing responsibility to another, Truman wanted people to know he accepted personal responsibility for the way the country was governed. He occasionally referred to his desk sign in public statements. In his farewell address in January of 1953, he said, "The President–whoever he is–has to decide. He can't pass the buck to anybody. No one else can do the deciding for him. That's his job."[1]

Truman believed in the solemnity of his role and responsibility, and although he worked within the limits of the Constitution, people regularly questioned the authority of his choices. Jesus had questions about his authority, too. After clearing the temple grounds of dishonest and greedy moneychangers, Jewish council leaders challenged his authoritative actions. However, they weren't prepared for Jesus' responses, nor his assertions of God's ultimate authority.

LUKE 20:1–8, 20–26

1 One day as he was teaching the people in the temple courts and preaching the gospel, the chief priests and the teachers of the law, together with the elders, came up to him. **2** "Tell us by what authority you are doing these things," they said. "Who gave you this authority?" **3** He replied, "I will also ask you a question. Tell me, **4** John's baptism—was it from heaven, or from men?" **5** They discussed it among themselves and said, "If we say, 'From heaven,' he will ask, 'Why didn't you believe him?' **6** But if we say, 'From men,' all the people will stone us, because they are persuaded that John was a prophet." **7** So they answered, "We don't know where it was from." **8** Jesus said, "Neither will I tell you by what authority I am doing these things."

•   •

20 Keeping a close watch on him, they sent spies, who pretended to be honest. They hoped to catch Jesus in something he said so that they might hand him over to the power and authority of the governor. **21** So the spies questioned him: "Teacher, we know that you speak and teach what is right, and that you do not show partiality but teach the way of God in accordance with the truth. **22** Is it right for us to pay taxes to Caesar or not?" **23** He saw through their duplicity and said to them, **24** "Show me a denarius. Whose portrait and inscription are on it?"

²⁵ "Caesar's," they replied. He said to them, "Then give to Caesar what is Caesar's, and to God what is God's." ²⁶ They were unable to trap him in what he had said there in public. And astonished by his answer, they became silent.

Who Said You Could? (20:1–8)

One day while Jesus was teaching and proclaiming the gospel in the temple courts, a delegation, upset by his recent purification of the temple, came to ask him by whose authority he had acted. The group was comprised of members of the Sanhedrin. They were the highest ruling body of the Jewish people in social and religious matters, and also held sole responsibility for regulating temple affairs (see sidebar). In their minds, only the promised Messiah could intrude as Jesus had, without their permission. Since they doubted his messiahship, they hoped their questions would trap and expose him as a religious fraud before the admirers who listened to him daily (see Luke 19:47).

By asking under whose authority Jesus was doing "these things" (20:2), they expressed emphatic displeasure with several of his actions: his interference in temple life, his forgiveness of sins (7:48–50), healing on the Sabbath (6:6–11; 14:1–6), demand of total allegiance (9:23–24), and scolding of them in the "woes" (11:37–54). They were upset by his teachings, acts of mercy, and miracles (4:16–24, 40–44; 6:1–5; 12:1–12; 19:1–7). As his actions increased his popularity with the people, religious leaders felt their influence over the multitudes threatened. Their question was therefore probably intended to arouse an outright messianic confession from Jesus by which they could accuse him of blasphemy. But he was not fooled by their deceit.

In response, Jesus used the commonly practiced debating pattern familiar in rabbinical methodology, by returning their question with one of his own. It was not an evasion, but rather, a subtle answer identifying his source of authority as the same as John the Baptist's. His response acknowledged that John didn't have *their* permission to teach and baptize; was Jesus therefore acting under God's ordination and commission or sinfully pretending to speak with God's authority? (cf. Acts 5:38–39).

This was a sore spot for the religious leaders, and Jesus knew it! His question publicly placed them in a theological, moral, and ethical dilemma. Their answer would clarify to him–and those observing their dialogue–their opinions about John the Baptist, but they didn't necessarily want their opinions revealed! Rather than offering an immediate response, they "discussed it among themselves" (Luke 20:5), realizing they needed to answer cautiously. If they said John acted as God's messenger, Jesus could certainly ask them why they had not believed or accepted him. Yet if they stated John acted on his own authority, they ran the risk of being stoned by surrounding listeners on the grounds of being false witness. Many of the people regarded John as a great prophet of God and had been baptized by him. The leaders' fear of stoning might be interpreted as merely hyperbole, similar to a teenager today saying, "My mom's going to kill me!" However, to some of the Jewish faithful, a denial of John the Baptist might actually have been worthy of death.

Laden with these fears, and cornered by Jesus, the leaders claimed ignorance. Before the surrounding crowd, they essentially elected to discredit themselves. As those who feigned complete authority in spiritual matters, they should have had wisdom enough to answer such a simple question about the veracity of a prophet. Choosing ignorance meant they were incompetent to serve as religious leaders on a matter of great importance.

Jesus perceived their insincerity and knew arguing with people motivated by bias and hostility would only invite more trouble. Fundamentally, his response in 20:8 was, "If you don't know authority when you see it, nothing I say will change your mind."

Show Me the Money (20:20–26)

Though silenced for the moment, the Sanhedrin was not ready to give up on their efforts to entrap Jesus. They still believed snaring him in his words was the route to bring about his destruction (cf. Luke 11:54). Whereas they'd tried disgracing Jesus before the people as a counterfeit prophet, their next ploy was to level accusations against him related to the Roman political regime.

In an effort to distance themselves from possible accusation and disapproval by the multitudes, the Sanhedrin watched Jesus closely, looking for patterns and opportune moments in which to lay their snare. When the time was ripe, they sent some of their disciples, not as an official delegation, but rather as a small group pretending (lit. *hypocrite*) to sincerely seek an answer to a question pertinent to most Jews. Luke described them as "spies" (Gr. *egkathetous*), a harsh word meaning *hired and sent secretly to trap* (20:20).

First, they flattered Jesus, implying they believed he alone could offer fair and truthful guidance, that his authority would settle the question once and for all. Possibly they hoped to make him think it was an ongoing dispute they'd had without finding answers from other Jewish leaders. They celebrated his impartiality (ironically, an attribute despised by those who sent them because Jesus demonstrated equity to tax-collectors and prostitutes), then lauded his teaching of the "way of God" (20:21; i.e. living in obedience to God's commands. cf. Isaiah 30:21, Genesis 18:19, Judges 2:22, Proverbs 10:29).

Their question pertained to a topic neither unfamiliar nor insignificant for their culture or ours–taxes. They wondered: Was it right or lawful (lit. *loosened*, meaning "does God's law have room") for the Jewish people to pay taxes to Caesar? Since 6 A.D., Rome had expected tribute from all provinces. It served as a consistent reminder to Jews of their subjection, and most perceived it as an insult to God, Israel's true ruler. Furthermore, when added to the standard religious taxes owed, Jews bore an estimated tax burden of 40 percent.[2]

The group intended the formation of their question to allow Jesus only a "yes" or "no" response. If "no," they could accuse him before outraged Roman authorities, if "yes," the spies assumed his esteem among the masses would be jeopardized or lost. Furthermore, for Jews who regarded him as the Messiah, or at least thought he might be, to endorse Rome's taxation was contrary to their perception of the Messiah as the one who would free them from oppressors and dominating principalities.

However, Jesus recognized their "duplicity" (lit. *craftiness*; Luke 20:23), and set the stage for their demise by asking for a denarius. Unlike some other coins which bore emblems from nature (crops, trees, etc.), the denarius, the equivalent of a day's wage to a laborer, bore the image and name of the emperor. Such coins usually included a claim of divinity for the emperor. This particularly disturbed some Jews who perceived human portraits on coinage as idolatry.

Jesus sought a deliberate and exact confession of these spies, asking, "Whose portrait and inscription are on it?" (20:24). This question invited public acknowledgment by his opponents of something those observing already knew: Caesar's image implied his ownership. First century inhabitants understood that a ruler's power generally extended to all areas where his/her money was used. Therefore, whether they liked it or not, Roman rule was clearly accepted as reality since Jews were using their coinage, even on temple grounds.

Jesus then masterfully instructed all those listening to "give to Caesar what is Caesar's, and to God what is God's" (20:25). He did not evade the question nor imply that discussions regarding the interaction of faith and the state are insignificant. Instead, he declared they should give the Roman government what was due them as their governing principality. The wording in Greek is simply "to give back."

Jesus carefully distinguished between Caesar and God. His mission was not politically driven; his kingdom was not of this world (John 18:36). While the coin bore the image of Caesar, and should therefore be surrendered to him on demand; human beings bear God's image, and should be unconditionally and wholly surrendered to his lordship. Jesus did not imply that God and Caesar are equals, poised on either end of a balance. God is the ultimate authority, deserving all honor, glory, faith, praise, and obedience. When coupled with Romans 13:1–5 and 1 Peter 2:13–14, believers can live confidently assured that obedience to governing authorities is, in fact, part of obedience to God, when not in conflict with divine instruction.

Jesus' challengers were astonished and silent. "Unable (lit. *lacking strength*) to trap him" (Luke 20:26) because of his great wisdom, they walked away with no ammunition for discrediting him before the Roman government. Once again deceitful men appeared foolish before the surrounding crowds.

God Told Me To

When challenged, Jesus did not respond with anger, malice, sarcasm, or defensiveness. With authority and wisdom, he simply spoke truth to all who challenged him; saying only what the Father desired (John 8:28; 12:50), and it ultimately cost him his life. Yet even in his death and resurrection he acted according to God's pleasure and his own authority (John 10:17–18), thus pointing to God's supremacy over all religious and civil leaders and laws.

Jesus' Jewish opponents in Luke 20 were not ready to die for their opinions. In contrast, within only weeks and years of these encounters, his followers were ready for persecution or death when questioned by authorities (see Peter and John, Acts 4:18–20; Stephen, Acts 6:8–8:1; Paul, Acts 25:1–11). Challenges, suffering, and martyrdom for Christ still occur. What questions are you facing today in life or from others that require the simple, gentle answer, "God told me to, and he is my authority"? Are you willing to pay the price for this truthful response? What is your level of commitment to your faith? Where are your greatest loyalties? Jesus did not allow the influence of any of the other leader(s) to override God's calling and supremacy in his thinking or his life. He would not allow their pride, self-preservation, or disapproval to derail his purposes. Will you resolve to "obey God rather than men" (Acts 5:29)?

THE SANHEDRIN

This council of 71 men, presided over by the high priest, served the first century Jewish community as a courtroom of authorities. Its inception, according to Jewish tradition, occurred when Moses called out 70 elders to share the burden of leadership (Numbers 11:16–25). Reorganized several times throughout Jewish history, by the time of Christ, it performed a considerably different function than in Moses' time and consisted of three groups:

- Chief Priests—men born of Aaron's lineage who served in the temple complex

- Teachers of the Law—men belonging to the rabbinical profession who served as scribes, instructors, interpreters of the law, and managed synagogues

- Elders—men who held no role in religious function or instruction, but were respected and distinguished in the community, often due to wealth

Within these three groups were also those who identified themselves as Sadducees or Pharisees. Commonly, the Sadducees were chief priests, and the Pharisees were teachers, but this was not rigid, since there were also varying sects within each group. Generally, the Sanhedrin acted with autonomy in private or temple matters, able to punish for minor crimes. Their inability to enact Jesus' death sentence without Roman approval indicates limits to their authority.

WHERE WILL IT LEAD?

Tom and Cindy are faithful members of their church, but they also enjoy instruction by other teachers for spiritual reflection and guidance. Sometimes these teachers press an issue or raise a thought that seems unorthodox to them. Should they continue following these individuals and overlook the problems? Why?

For Personal Reflection:

- Identify your spiritual/religious leaders. Are they denominational or local church staff? Bible study teachers? Spiritual mentors? Godly friends?

Christian writers/speakers? How do they help or hinder the work of Christ? Consider what makes them good to follow. Or are they?

- Jesus never expected people to simply accept him at face value. He said he'd come to fulfill the law and the prophets (Matthew 5:17), inviting people to check out his claims. Do the people you follow point you to the Way, the Truth, and the Life?

QUESTIONS

1. When have you been in a situation in which authorities (secular or religious) did not understand your choices or actions? What were your motives? Were you prevented from acting in accordance with your beliefs?

2. What questions can only be answered with God's authority? In a world that often denies the existence of absolute truth, how can we offer God's word and wisdom as authoritative? Can we help those around us without Christ accept God's authority through any means other than faith?

3. Jesus' authoritative teaching threatened the religious leaders' power and influence over the people. Are you threatened by it as well? If so, what particular areas of control do you struggle to surrender?

4. Jesus *owed* obedience to no one. In the incarnation, he took "the very nature of a servant" (Philippians 2:7), and willingly submitted himself to the laws and authorities of his day. But he was still completely authoritative over all creation (e.g. calming the sea, forgiving sin, healing the sick, raising the dead). How does his balance between submission and authority affect your interaction with him and other authorities in your life?

5. The desire to challenge authority seems inherent in most every person (consider a 2-year old, a teenager, or a grumpy old man or woman). Do you think this is a part of humanity's sin nature or from being created in the image of God?

6. Have you ever left a challenging conversation thinking, "I should have said . . ." or wishing you'd said something differently or more cleverly? In these situations, was it that you lacked the authority you thought you had (pride), or did you not exert the authority you were truly given (insecurity)? What do you think Jesus' emotions were during and after verbal confrontations like these found in Luke 20?

N O T E S ──────────────────────────────

1. See "The Buck Stops Here Desk Sign" at http://www.trumanlibrary.org/buckstop.htm. Accessed 2/19/2013.

2. John Nolland, "Luke 18:35—24:53," *Word Biblical Commentary*, vol. 35C; Accordance/Thomas Nelson electronic ed. (Waco: Word Books, 1993, 2006), 958.

LESSON ELEVEN

Questions about the Future

MAIN IDEA

Jesus used a comment about the temple as a springboard to prepare his disciples for the future.

QUESTION TO EXPLORE

How should we prepare for the future?

STUDY AIM

To prepare myself to face the future with faith rather than fear

QUICK READ

Jesus' disciples asked him questions about the future. His replies created more uncertainties than answers, but were lined with encouragement and assurances of hope, protection, and victory.

In the movie *Back to the Future, Part II,* using the time machine he built from a DeLorean, Professor Emmett Brown (Doc), flies to the future (2015) then returns to 1985 to break some bad news to his time-traveling teenage companion Marty McFly. Marty's future as an adult hangs in jeopardy because of foolish choices. Doc's intent is to help Marty ensure a positive future–without divulging too much–which could (potentially) destroy the time-space continuum. Marty desperately desires to know specifics, and begs, "Tell me about my future. I know I make it big, but do I become, like, a rich rock star?" Instead of giving the details Marty wants, Doc explains why he can't: "Please Marty. No one should know too much about their destiny."[1] Apparently, Jesus felt the same way! When people asked questions about the coming days, he gave no specifics, but explained *why* things would happen as they would.

LUKE 21:5–24

[5] Some of his disciples were remarking about how the temple was adorned with beautiful stones and with gifts dedicated to God. But Jesus said, [6] "As for what you see here, the time will come when not one stone will be left on another; every one of them will be thrown down." [7] "Teacher," they asked, "when will these things happen? And what will be the sign that they are about to

take place?" **8** He replied: "Watch out that you are not deceived. For many will come in my name, claiming, 'I am he,' and, 'The time is near.' Do not follow them. **9** When you hear of wars and revolutions, do not be frightened. These things must happen first, but the end will not come right away." **10** Then he said to them: "Nation will rise against nation, and kingdom against kingdom. **11**There will be great earthquakes, famines and pestilences in various places, and fearful events and great signs from heaven. **12** "But before all this, they will lay hands on you and persecute you. They will deliver you to synagogues and prisons, and you will be brought before kings and governors, and all on account of my name. **13** This will result in your being witnesses to them. **14**But make up your mind not to worry beforehand how you will defend yourselves. **15** For I will give you words and wisdom that none of your adversaries will be able to resist or contradict. **16** You will be betrayed even by parents, brothers, relatives and friends, and they will put some of you to death. **17** All men will hate you because of me. **18** But not a hair of your head will perish. **19** By standing firm you will gain life. **20** "When you see Jerusalem being surrounded by armies, you will know that its desolation is near. **21** Then let those who are in Judea flee to the mountains, let those in the city get out, and let those in the country not enter the city. **22** For this is the time of punishment in fulfillment of all that has been written. **23** How dreadful it will be in those days for pregnant women and nursing mothers! There will be great distress in the land and wrath against this people. ²⁴ They will fall by the sword and will be taken as prisoners to all the nations. Jerusalem will be trampled on by the Gentiles until the times of the Gentiles are fulfilled."

Expect the Unexpected (21:5–11)

Herod's temple was a grand and glorious complex of buildings, sculptures, 40-foot columns, porches, court-yards, towers, staircases, and gates surrounded by an imposing series of walls. Massive stones (some the size of a Volkswagen Beetle) were used in its construction and many surfaces were plated with gold or silver. Its grandeur was tremendous. When Herod the Great became king in 37 B.C., he determined building up the temple would engender loyalty from the Jews while simultaneously impressing the Romans. Even in Jesus' day, the complex was still undergoing construction and change (it wasn't completed until 64 A.D.), as people continuously brought valuable offerings (e.g. tapestries, gold and bronze fix-tures, and art) as gifts dedicated to God.

Therefore, it seemed natural after Jesus celebrated the poor widow's gift (Luke 21:3–4), that the conversa-tion with his followers turned to the beauty of the temple she, they, and countless others were helping to fund. Skimming past Jesus' point about sacrificial giving, they focused on the tangible, observable, and amazing temple. (Surely it was worth more of their time and energy than a couple of coins?!) That's why they were stunned to hear the temple's destruction was imminent. How could such a massive structure of spiritual significance, immense wealth, prestige, and beauty possibly be demolished? Though some interpret this passage as referencing the end of time, Jesus specifically referred to the temple's destruction–"As for what you see here" (21:6)–which occurred in 70 A.D., when the Romans crushed a Jewish revolt, leaving Jerusalem in ruins.[2] Furthermore, "the time will come" (21:6) is identified as a prophetic pronouncement because of its frequent use in introducing a message from God. As such, it announced a specific future event, not a general time period (cf. Jeremiah 7:32, 19:6; Amos 8:11).

For the moment, however, Jesus' disciples stood shocked at the news of the temple's demise. The temple's grandeur had, in effect, lulled them into a false sense of security about their condition and well-being. As long as the temple stood, they reasoned, God's favor still rested on his people. The Messiah would have a grand structure from which to stage his overthrow of their oppressors and their hope for autonomy and freedom lived (see sidebar). For Jesus to announce the temple's destruction was tantamount to proclaiming the death of the Jewish nation. Thus, they immediately sought details about this fearful and drastic prediction, wondering what signs would reveal its occurrence and when it would take place.

Although they asked "when," Jesus instead answered with "why." To endure the coming days, they would need strong, true faith in him alone. Knowing that deception challenges and even destroys faith, Jesus first warned the disciples that before the temple's fall, there would be false prophets (e.g. Acts 13:5–12, 20:28–31; 2 Corinthians 11:1–15). Messianic types would also arise claiming to be the Messiah, claiming to act under Messiah's authority, or claiming to be representative of Jesus' presence.[3] Their message "the time is near" (Luke 21:8) might be interpreted two ways: 1) that the temple's destruction indicated the nearness of the end of time, or 2) that the time for rising up against political and religious authorities had come. Regardless of interpretation, Jesus instructed his disciples not to follow their leadership. The inclusion of this restriction is unique to Luke. Although parallel passages in Matthew 24:1–25 and Mark 13:1–23, known as the Olivet Discourse, do not specifically forbid following these charlatans, all three passages instruct believers to "flee to the mountains" (Luke 21:21), implying separation from these fraudulent leaders.

Despite the news of "wars and revolutions" (21:9), which Jesus' followers recognized as standard prophetic images; they were not to fear, nor think the end of the age had yet arrived. Jesus assured his followers God's sovereignty was still intact, for this chaos was neither random nor accidental, but all part of a divine plan. These uprisings did in fact occur in the form of revolts and internal conflicts among the Romans during the reigns of Nero and Vespasian (54–79 A.D.), and were in partial fulfillment of the prophetic promises Jesus spoke in 21:7–24.[4]

Luke introduced Jesus' next words in 21:10 with, "then he said to them," another prophetic pronouncement (cf. Isaiah 37:6; Jeremiah 42:9). The multiple prophecies which followed were observed and recorded historically before the temple's demise. These included: famines during the reigns of Claudius (41–54 A.D.; cf. Acts 11:28) and Nero (54–68 A.D.), a severe earthquake in Phrygia in 61 A.D., and the eruption of Vesuvius in 63 A.D., leaving Pompeii in ruins. In addition, a comet in the form of a sword appeared over Jerusalem every night for a considerable time in 66 A.D. (now believed to be Halley's Comet); and in 68 A.D., the Jewish rebellion against Rome began, which ultimately led to Jerusalem's destruction in 70 A.D.

It's Gonna Get Personal (21:12–19)

However, before these escalating difficulties began, Jesus warned his followers to expect personal challenges. His disciples would experience persecution similar to his own looming suffering. Although the persecutors were not specifically named, it is clear both Jewish and Gentile authorities would oppress them. The faithful were delivered to "synagogues" for interrogation, and to "prisons" for punishment (Luke 21:12). They stood before "kings and governors" because of their confession of Christ and had opportunity to testify of their Savior.[5]

Despite these fearful predictions, Jesus encouraged his disciples to be confident and hopeful, deciding ahead of time to not worry about explanations if summoned before authorities. Knowing human nature as he did, Jesus presumed at least some of his followers might outline their defense in a polished, orderly presentation (maybe using the first-century equivalent of PowerPoint, too!) Instead, he promised to provide the wise words needed for the moment (cf. John 16:13–15; Acts 4:29; 6:10). Furthermore, adversaries would be unable to refute them, just as Sanhedrin delegates were silenced by Jesus (see Luke 20:7, 26). This certainly did not mean acquittal in every instance, because some of Jesus' followers were executed through the betrayal of loved ones. This would be distressing news to anyone, but was paralleled in Christ's life through Judas' kiss.

Hatred would have no restrictions. Christ's followers could expect animosity on all fronts. Nevertheless, he promised to sustain them. It seems contradictory for Jesus to say some would die (21:16) then claim, "not a hair of your head will perish" (21:18). The latter was actually a Hebrew idiom representing total deliverance from a dangerous situation (cf. 1 Samuel 14:45; 2 Samuel 14:11; 1 Kings 1:52). As believers stood firm (lit. "endurance") they would find safety for their souls (cf. John 10:28; Philippians 1:21; Acts 27:34; Romans 8:37–39).

The End of the [City] as We Know It (21:20–24)

After the interlude of Luke 21:12–19, Jesus resumed speaking about what to expect after the escalating events of 21:11. Whereas Jesus' initial warnings were about the temple, his continued prophecies regarded the demise of the whole of Jerusalem.

As Gentile armies surrounded (lit. "encircle") Jerusalem, disciples must take heed, understanding the nearness of the city's destruction,[6] and they should flee to the mountains. Like many of Jesus' teachings, this contradicted traditional patterns. Commonly, people fled to walled cities for protection, not away from them. However, Jesus knew the city was doomed, therefore, walls would only serve to capture, not preserve them. The nearest mountains were on the other side of the Jordan River. Pella, one of the Greek Decapolis towns in the mountains south of the Sea of Galilee, became home to most of the Christian refugees from Jerusalem during the Jewish revolution and Roman subjugation. For those expecting Jesus to overthrow the Roman political regime in Judea, the instruction to run away completely opposed the call to arms they expected.

Jerusalem's capture fulfilled Scriptural judgment prophecies as the "time of punishment" (lit. "vengeance;" 21:22) upon rebellious Jews who rejected God's Son. It was the out-pouring of God's wrath, not simply a volitional act of political forces. The Roman army was merely God's instrument to bring about chastisement. Jesus warned this period of time would be so dreadful, something as joyful as motherhood would be dimmed by the horror. The vulnerable states of those pregnant or nursing would be distressing and even dangerous for survival, because of the inability to move quickly or hide easily.

For those who ignored the warnings to flee Jerusalem and its vicinity, death or exile was certain. In 70 A.D. this prophecy became reality. Titus, son of Emperor Vespasian, led a five-month siege of Jerusalem at which time the Roman army overtook and plundered the city. They killed thousands of Jews, specifically the old and infirm. Then they exiled the remaining residents, so that not a single Jew was left alive in Jerusalem.

This prediction of the city's fall to pagan nations grieved Jesus' listeners. The experience of these incredible disasters and seeing God's wrath poured out on unrighteousness was nevertheless lined with a glimmer of hope: the word "until" (21:24). Christ assured them the godless Gentile nations who would control Jerusalem (see sidebar) would also receive judgment when the Son of Man returned to establish his eternal kingdom (21:27–28).

Knowing Who Holds Tomorrow

Perhaps you too have asked the Lord "when" questions and he's answered with "why." For his disciples listening pre–70

A.D., Jesus' prophecies about the future were terrifying, but his words were intended (and needed) to encourage faith, challenge confidence, and breed hope. He broadened their perspective to include issues greater than the temple and a future bigger than their understanding.

Jesus' perspective is always bigger than we envision. He sees the end from the beginning, and desires we place our confidence in him and his word (Psalm 119:105). As disciples on this side of 70 A.D., his words still challenge us to believe, by faith, that he is greater than anything we will face in the future. Despite struggles and persecutions, because he is God incarnate, we can look to the future with faith, resting in promises such as Isaiah 46:9–10:

> *Remember the former things, those of long ago;*
> *I am God, and there is no other;*
> *I am God, and there is none like me.*
> *I make known the end from the beginning, from ancient times, what is still to come.*
> *I say: My purpose will stand, and I will do all that I please.*

WHY CAN'T WE KEEP IT?

Couldn't God's plan have included saving the temple despite Jerusalem's fall? Wouldn't it be great to still have all the stones where Jesus walked, the courtyards where he sat and taught, and the gates at which he healed? Certainly, but couldn't those very sites become idols?

That's apparently what had happened for the Jews in Jesus' day. Although they didn't believe God's presence was predicated by the temple or existed exclusively within it, Jews thought religion apart from the temple was unlikely, if not impossible (cf. Jer. 7:1–15). "Temple" simply means *sacred* or *holy space.* Jesus came to bring a new covenant and means by which to worship (John 4:23–24), and our bodies are now the Holy Spirit's temple (1 Corinthians 6:19). Is your life proof that the "the old has gone, the new has come!" (2 Corinthians 5:17), or do you cling to idols of tradition and familiarity?

GENTILES IN JERUSALEM

For years after Jerusalem's destruction, Jews were not allowed in the city or its environs except one day annually to commemorate the temple. Even then, they were only permitted to mourn from hills overlooking Jerusalem. The first Jews finally permitted to inhabit the city again were Christian descendants of those who fled to Pella.

In 132 A.D., Jews in Jerusalem staged a revolution against the Romans. Emperor Hadrian saw the city taken and destroyed, this time resolving to make it exclusively pagan, renaming it *Aelia Capitolina* and building a shrine where the temple had stood. Although briefly transformed to Christianity under Constantine, Muslims conquered Jerusalem in 637 A.D., and built the Dome of the Rock Mosque on the temple mount. Jesus' prediction of Gentile domination is still in fulfillment.

QUESTIONS

1. Like the disciples in Luke 21:7–8, what "when" questions have you asked Jesus and he answered with "why" instead?

2. Why do you think the disciples were looking for a sign (21:7) to indicate the "when" of the temple's destruction?

3. What future event in your own life fills you with uncertainty or fear? How can you exercise faith and cling to hope?

4. Clearly, there are some parts of the future Jesus intends to remain a mystery for humanity. Is there a particular area of your future for which you would like to see a preview? Are there some areas of your past you're glad you didn't know about ahead of time?

NOTES ────────────────────────────────

1. *Back to the Future, Part II*. Dir. Robert Zemeckis. Perf. Michael J. Fox, Christopher Lloyd and Lea Thompson. Universal Pictures, Amblin Entertainment and U-Drive Productions, 1989.

2. Jesus stated in Luke 21:6, "not one stone will be left on another." Any visitor to Jerusalem or student of history knows that a few of those stones still stand on one another in the form of the modern day "Wailing Wall," used by thousands as a place of prayer. Jesus intended this as hyperbole to communicate the immensity of the devastation to occur.

3. The words Jesus said they would use, "I am he" (Lit. "I am"; Gr. *ego eimi*) are the same words Jesus used to describe himself in John 4:26; 6:35; 6:48; 8:12, 58; 9:5; 11:25; 14:6 which all parallel Exodus 3:14 where God says "I am." Thus, these false leaders will be claiming divine authority, character, or representation.

4. *Prophetic promises* (where God works through agents already present in everyday history) are contrasted with *apocalyptic imagery* (describing God breaking into history in a marvelous way), which Jesus used in Luke 21:25–38. See Darrell L. Bock, *The NIV Application Commentary: Luke* (Grand Rapids, MI: Zondervan, 1996), 532.

5. In Acts 4–12, Luke recorded these earliest persecutions as Jesus predicted in Luke 21:12: Peter and John before the Sanhedrin; the apostles arrested, imprisoned and beaten; Stephen stoned; Saul persecuting believers; and James executed by Herod. Paul also enumerated his struggles in 2 Corinthians 11:23–27. Tradition records all the apostles (except John) died a violent death either from Jewish or secular authorities. Relatives and friends accused believers of blasphemy because they claimed Jesus was the resurrected Messiah. Nero tortured Christians in Rome where pagans reported believers who would not worship the emperor. All this occurred before the temple's destruction.

6. The parallel passages of Matthew 24:15–16 and Mark 13:14 use the term "abomination that causes desolation," an allusion to the prophecies of Daniel 9:27; 11:31 and 12:11. Luke presumably omitted "abomination" to keep from confusing Jerusalem's fall with the end times, and for the sake of his Gentile readers who wouldn't grasp the familiarity of the phrase.

LESSON TWELVE

*Questions about
Jesus' Identity*

MAIN IDEA

Jesus responded to questions about his identity by verifying that he was a King and the Son of God.

QUESTION TO EXPLORE

Who is Jesus?

STUDY AIM

To affirm Jesus' identity as King and the Son of God; and to submit myself to his leadership

QUICK READ

Despite his divine and authoritative identity, Jesus willingly surrendered his life to, and for, people who didn't believe his claims. My surrender to him reflects what I believe about him.

I have a great excuse when I lose something around the house. I simply tell my husband the "real" Julie has it with her, so I'm not at fault. Apparently, the "real" Julie also has my "real" (i.e. original) birth certificate.

This all stems from an identity crisis I had a few years ago. I'd gone to get a passport, taking the necessary documentation with me. To my surprise, the government worker processing my application announced my birth certificate wasn't an original; it was a copy. I didn't know official certificates usually have a raised seal or embossed stamp. I'd simply taken the same piece of paper my parents used to enroll me in school, get my driver's license, and other important things.

For a split-second in that government office, I wondered, "Am I *really* Julie?!" Despite more than three decades of verifying my identity, that certificate was now useless, and no matter how adamantly I insisted, the employee needed genuine proof.[1]

Despite the evidence of his words and actions, many of those Jesus encountered during his trials had cold hearts, closed minds, and insecurities that prevented them from believing in him as Messiah. Under the guise of demanding further proof and testimony of his identity, they twisted his words to discount his claims and demean his character. The Son of God underwent intense scrutiny about his identity, but he nevertheless welcomes those who ask him, "Who are you?" in hopes they will surrender to him.

LUKE 22:66–71

66 At daybreak the council of the elders of the people, both the chief priests and teachers of the law, met together, and Jesus was led before them. **67** "If you are the Christ, " they said, "tell us." Jesus answered, "If I tell you, you will not believe me, **68** and if I asked you, you would not answer.**69** But from now on, the Son of Man will be seated at the right hand of the mighty God." **70** They all asked, "Are you then the Son of God?" He replied, "You are right in saying I am." **71** Then they said, "Why do we need any more testimony? We have heard it from his own lips."

LUKE 23:1–25

1 Then the whole assembly rose and led him off to Pilate. **2** And they began to accuse him, saying, "We have found this man subverting our nation. He opposes payment of taxes to Caesar and claims to be Christ, a king." **3** So Pilate asked Jesus, "Are you the king of the Jews?" "Yes, it is as you say," Jesus replied. **4** Then Pilate announced to the chief priests and the crowd, "I find no basis for a charge against this man." **5** But they insisted, "He stirs up the people all over Judea by his teaching. He started in Galilee and has come all the way here." **6** On hearing this, Pilate asked if the man was a Galilean. **7** When he learned that Jesus was under Herod's jurisdiction, he sent him to Herod, who was also in Jerusalem at that time. **8** When Herod saw Jesus, he was greatly pleased, because for a long time he had been wanting to see him. From what he had heard about him, he hoped to see him perform some miracle. **9** He plied him with many questions, but Jesus gave him no answer. **10** The chief priests and the teachers of the law were standing there, vehemently accusing him. **11** Then Herod and his soldiers ridiculed and mocked him. Dressing him in an elegant robe, they sent him back to Pilate. **12** That day Herod and Pilate became friends—before this they had been enemies. **13** Pilate called together the chief priests, the rulers and the people, **14** and said to them, "You brought me this man as one who was inciting the people to rebellion. I have examined him in your presence and have found no basis for your charges against him. **15** Neither has Herod, for he sent him back to us; as you can see, he has done nothing to deserve death. **16** Therefore, I will punish him and then release him. " **18** With one voice they cried out, "Away with this man! Release Barabbas to us!" **19** (Barabbas had been thrown into prison for an insurrection in the city, and for murder.) **20** Wanting to release Jesus, Pilate appealed to them again. **21** But they kept shouting, "Crucify him! Crucify him!" **22** For the third time he spoke to them: "Why? What crime has this man committed? I have found in him no grounds for the death penalty. Therefore I will have him punished and then release him." **23** But with loud shouts they insistently demanded that he be crucified, and their shouts prevailed. **24** So Pilate decided to grant their demand. **25** He released the man who had been thrown into prison for insurrection and murder, the one they asked for, and surrendered Jesus to their will.

Who Are You? (22:66—23:7)

Throughout the night hours, away from the public eye, Jesus was betrayed, arrested, mocked, and beaten (Luke 22:48, 52, 63). As morning dawned, the Sanhedrin,[2] the highest ruling body of the Jews in social and religious matters, interrogated him. They sought not to determine truth, but rather to find means by which to take him before the Roman government or condemn him before the Jewish people. Given Jesus' popularity with the masses, they opted for a political agenda. They focused on his identity, knowing his disciples claimed him as the Messiah or Christ (Matthew 16:16; John 1:41; 11:27) and a king (Luke 19:38; John 1:49). It was a prudent choice, considering how the Romans feared insurrection. If the Sanhedrin could jointly testify that Jesus himself used these titles, Pilate (see sidebar) would be obliged to execute him as a danger to Caesar's authority in Israel. So to get a confession, they asked Jesus if he was the Christ. Knowing they only wanted something to use against him and weren't sincerely seeking to dialogue, Jesus avoided a straightforward answer. His interrogators included those who had asked him about his authority in the temple (see Luke 20:1–8). His answer certainly reminded them of their inability to respond before, and acknowledged their unwillingness to answer him now. Imagine their frustration and rage!

Jesus' continuing apologetic prophesied his coming resurrection and exaltation. Using two Old Testament passages accepted as messianic prophecies, 22:69 draws from Daniel 7:13 in which a "son of man" [3] appeared in divine revelation and rule, and Psalm 110:1 where the Lord was instructed to sit at God's "right hand." When Jesus said the Son of Man would be seated "at the right hand of the mighty God" (Luke 22:69), he meant an entrance into God's glory; a vision Stephen saw in fruition a short time later (see Acts 7:54–56). By using these references, Jesus inferred his divinity and equality with God. So they asked him pointedly, "Are you then the Son of God?" (Luke 22:70). Jesus' reply incorporated the unique "I am" identifier God gave himself in Exodus 3:14. This provided the Sanhedrin fodder for building their case against Jesus with the Jewish multitudes. They cast him not as a hero, but as a blasphemer, worthy of death according to the Law (see Leviticus 24:16).

This claim of divinity was still not the confession of political subversion they'd been looking for, but it was close enough to be twisted for Roman ears. Although Tiberius Caesar was not adamant about it, emperors generally perceived themselves as divine, so Jesus' claim could be considered competitive with Caesar's power and authority. Believing this was the ammunition they needed against Jesus, they took him to Pilate, the Roman prefect over Judea from 26–36 A.D. Under Tiberius' authority, Pilate handled the region's civil, legal, and political administration, which is why the Sanhedrin sought his approval of Jesus' execution. Luke possibly used hyperbole to say the "whole" assembly rose and led Jesus to Pilate (Luke 23:1). He knew at least two members, Nicodemus and Joseph of Arimathea, held an affinity for Jesus (see John 19:38–42; Luke 23:50–51; Matt. 27:57). However, these two men may not have been invited to the interrogation. If they were, they may have gone along as silent disciples, not condoning the Council's actions, but choosing to observe. Since it was still early morning, the multitudes had not yet learned of the night's events and therefore were not present to support, rescue, or defend Jesus.

Before Pilate, the Sanhedrin "accuse(d)," the legal term for bringing charges in a court of law, "this man" (an emphatic, derogatory reference), of "subverting" (lit. *perverting)* the Jews' loyalty to Caesar, lying to incriminate him[4] (Luke 23:2). Presenting him as "Messiah" to a Gentile ruler would have little effect, so they politicized the title and labeled it as royalty, which matched their understanding and interpretation of Scripture. Pilate likely suspected foul play from the Sanhedrin. Why else would men who *hated* Roman rule come to him complaining Jesus wanted to *overthrow* Roman rule? So Pilate asked Jesus if he was the king of the Jews, and although Jesus answered affirmatively, Pilate was unconvinced of his actual threat to Roman power.

After this interview, for the first of three times in the narrative, Pilate announced to the Sanhedrin and gathering crowd (see John 18:28–38; Matt. 27:17; Mark 15:8–11), he believed Jesus innocent (Luke 23:4). Whether he sincerely sought justice or just wanted to be done with the case, this pronouncement should have been official and final, resulting in Jesus' release. However, the Jewish leaders insisted Jesus was a troublemaker for the Roman Empire.

Jesus certainly drew attention as he traveled, healed, and taught throughout Israel, but his message was never rebellious or treasonous. The only truth these men presented was that Jesus began his teaching in Galilee![5] At the word "Galilee" (23:5), Pilate found an escape clause; he jumped at the opportunity to pass the responsibility for dealing with Jesus to the leader responsible for the region where this problem began.

What Will You Do? (23:8–12)

When using the four Gospels in concert, we learn Jesus' identity was scrutinized multiple times throughout the night. First, Luke 22:54 and John 18:12–24 report an interview with Annas, a former high priest with great influence and father-in-law of the current high priest. Secondly, Caiaphas and the Sanhedrin examined him (Matt. 26:57–68; Mark 14:53–65; John 18:24). A final trial before the Jewish authorities took place after daylight, as required by Jewish law in order for judgments to be formally accepted (Matt. 27:1; Mark 15:1; Luke 22:66—23:1; John 18:24). Jesus next stood before Pilate (Matt. 27:11–26; Mark 15:2–15; John 18:28—19:16). Luke alone included Jesus' audience before Herod (Luke 23:8–11).

Herod, as ruler of Galilee (see sidebar), knew of Jesus' ministry and miracles in his region and desired to see him, not to hear his message, but to observe a miracle "magic show." However, Jesus did not reply to his many questions, a fulfillment of Isaiah 53:7. In lieu of his silence, the Sanhedrin "vehemently"[6] (Luke 23:10) accused him.

Their words didn't convince Herod of Jesus' guilt. Since Jesus was in Jerusalem, and no longer a liability to him in Galilee, Herod decided Jesus' popularity with the masses wasn't worth the risk to his own reputation, so he chose to avoid judgment. Rather than declaring Jesus guilty or innocent, he thought it would appease the Sanhedrin and salve his own offense at Jesus' silence, to ridicule the prisoner. Herod and his soldiers mockingly dressed him in a purple robe (one used by royalty or high authorities on formal occasions) and returned Jesus to Pilate.

Oddly enough, this experience brought friendship between Herod and Pilate where there had previously been enmity. Apparently, Pilate's deference to Herod's role and authority, and their similar opinions about the situation, brought a new cooperation between them. Unfortunately for Pilate, Jesus' fate was left to him to decide.

What Has He Done? (23:13–25)

Upon Jesus' return, Pilate called together the Jewish leaders and people. He restated their accusations, assured them of his thorough examination (lit. *up and down judging*) before them, and announced (for the second time) his belief in Jesus' innocence. He emphatically added that Herod (a ruler with ideologies closer to theirs than his own) had found no reason to execute this man. Therefore, as a concession, he would have Jesus beaten and released.[7]

Instead of conceding to Pilate's suggestion, the people cried out for Jesus' execution and demanded the immediate release of Barabbas, a Jewish man convicted of insurrection and murder. Parallel passages in Matt. 27:15–22, Mark 15:6–15, and John 18:39–40 indicate the Roman government traditionally released one prisoner at Passover as a goodwill gesture to the Jews. Possibly the crowd demanded Barabbas' release because they hoped he would continue his anti-Roman efforts, but it seems likely the Jewish leadership worked tirelessly to defame Jesus before the people.[8] Perhaps some of the crowd hoped to force Jesus into miraculous and dramatic behaviors in order to free himself and overthrow the Roman yoke as their political Messiah-figure. Finally, we must acknowledge the reality of Luke 22:53; supernatural and evil forces were at work (Luke 22:3; John 14:30–31).

Pilate, uncharacteristic of a Roman magistrate, sought acquittal for Jesus. But the crowd shouted back all the more, demanding Jesus' crucifixion. Then for the third time, Pilate insisted on Jesus' innocence and demanded to understand why they desired his death. He reiterated he would punish Jesus and release him; however, the crowd's loud cries prevailed. Pilate capitulated; never conceding Jesus' guilt, but to avoid anarchy, he released the criminal from punishment and condemned the innocent one to death.

Surrender

The theme of surrender is richly pictured in Jesus' passion. He willingly surrendered his preferences to God's will (John 10:17–18; Luke 22:42), then surrendered himself to the guards at his arrest (Luke 22:52). The Sanhedrin surrendered him to Pilate for examination and sentencing (23:1–2), who then surrendered him to Herod (23:7). Herod surrendered his authority over the situation back to Pilate (23:11) who surrendered truth and justice to the demands of the crowd (23:23–24), and ultimately, Jesus to the Jews (23:25).

Daily, we make decisions concerning surrender. We surrender one priority to another: delaying house cleaning in order to mow the grass; eating a carrot instead of cake; instead of surfing the Internet, spending time with family; exercising instead of sleeping in; reading our Bibles before reading the news. While we may effectively keep our priorities in order, do we surrender Jesus to our wills, instead of surrendering our wills to Jesus? Our level of surrender reveals our fundamental beliefs about Jesus. Is he the Son of God to be worshipped and King to be served and obeyed, or merely a sacrificial lamb for our sins? Perhaps you're still trying to decide. What will your life today reflect about his identity?

PILATE THE PREFECT

Although Caesarea was the seat of Roman government for the region, Pilate was in Jerusalem for Passover because it was politically wise to be present. During this important Jewish festival, which celebrated cultural heritage and victories, Romans feared insurrection. History records Pilate as anti-Semitic, often looking for opportunities to instigate the Jews to rebel. His insistence that "King of the Jews" remain on the cross (John 19:19–22) was sarcastic mockery, as if to say, "this is the best royalty the Jews can produce." In 36 A.D., he was recalled to Rome for excessive cruelty toward Jewish civilians and removed from office.

HEROD ANTIPAS

King Herod the Great, with Roman government approval, granted his son Herod (Antipas) his position and title. Although his ancestors were Jewish proselytes, Jews viewed Herod as a foreigner, because his family came from Edom, southeast of the Dead Sea. In an attempt to gain their favor, he celebrated Jewish festivals, which was why he was in Jerusalem for Passover. At one point, Herod feared Jesus was John the Baptist resurrected (see Mark 6:16; Luke 13:31). In 39 A.D., Emperor Caligula sent Herod into exile on allegations of conspiracy.

PUT YOURSELF IN HIS SANDALS

Imagine you're Joseph of Arimathea, a prominent member of the Sanhedrin (Mark 15:43) and secret disciple (John 19:38), present at Christ's trials. Consider the following:

- What about your observations of Jesus in those early morning events helps or hinders your faith?

- What do you think and say during the proceedings?

- What do you expect or hope for Jesus to do or say?

- How do you respond to those shouting for Jesus' execution?

- Do you boldly call out for Barabbas' execution and Jesus' release?

- Do you try to conceal your entry into Pilate's palace to ask for Jesus' dead body (Matt. 27:58)?

By burying Jesus in a tomb he owned, Joseph revealed his discipleship and probably forever abandoned his place in the Sanhedrin. Are you willing to risk your place of status or influence for Jesus' sake? Do you believe in his identity that whole-heartedly? Does your surrender to God's will stretch that far?

QUESTIONS

1. In the description of Jesus' passion, many people find themselves in the story. Whether in opposition (the Jewish leaders), impartial indifference (Pilate), curiosity (Herod), disbelief of his identity (the crowd), or in silent fear (Jesus' followers). Do you find yourself reflected in any of these people? Whom and why?

2. Is your will fully surrendered to Jesus or does your life reveal his identity as something less than king in your daily choices?

3. What (if any) ramifications may have resulted if Jesus had performed miracles for Herod?

4. When, like Pilate, have you capitulated to popular opinion or avoided further controversy against your better judgment?

5. If you had to briefly explain Jesus' identity to someone who's never heard of him, what would you say?

NOTES

1. I'm happy to report the state of Alabama provided an "authentic" certificate in plenty of time, and I obtained my passport to make our trip overseas!

2. See Lesson 10 Sidebar, p. 155–156 for a more in-depth look at the Sanhedrin.

3. "Son of man" was Jesus' favorite self-designation. By using the phrase, he was able to avoid frequent public use of the label "Messiah," which helped limit controversial confrontations.

4. Specifically, the group claimed Jesus forbid Jews from paying Roman taxes. This was an outright lie, since Jesus stated Caesar should get what was rightly due him (see Luke 20:20–26).

5. Though born in Bethlehem of Judea, Jesus was raised in the Galilean town of Nazareth. He began his ministry there, expanding to Samaria and gradually moving toward Jerusalem. Contrast that with his instructions to the disciples in Acts 1:8: they were to begin in Jerusalem and extend out into the rest of the world!

6. The Greek *eutonos* (vehemently) has implications of bellowing or shrieking, conjuring images of Matt. 12:34 where Jesus called this same group of men a brood of vipers.

7. The beating Pilate advocated was less severe than "scourging" which used a whip plaited from strips of leather enlaced with knots and/or pieces of metal. Although this torture usually preceded crucifixion, it was sometimes fatal in and of itself. Perhaps Pilate hoped the multitudes might rise up in sympathy to defend Jesus since because of them even the Jewish authorities had reservations about harming him.

8. It is, perhaps, the Sanhedrin who actually "subverted" and "incited" the people (cf. Luke 23:2, 14).

LESSON THIRTEEN

Questions about the Promised Messiah

MAIN IDEA

Jesus confirmed his resurrection by explaining the Scriptures and revealing himself as the promised Messiah.

QUESTION TO EXPLORE

How do we need Jesus to reveal himself to us?

STUDY AIM

To find hope through conversations with Jesus and revelation from his word

QUICK READ

Using Scripture, Jesus spoke to the hearts of two despondent disciples. He revealed himself as alive and well, and the answer to the hope they'd lost.

All hope seemed lost. Jesus' arrest apparently prevented a major overthrow of the Roman government. His torture and crucifixion made him seem impotent and implausible as Messiah. His subsequent death appeared to be the end of the kingdom he'd promised to establish and the redemption of Israel he'd guaranteed. His life, his healing, his miracles, and his teaching all seemed to be buried with him in a tomb guarded by Roman soldiers.

For three days, Jesus' followers languished in disappointment, even despair. They feared being identified as one of his disciples (Luke 22:54–59; John 20:19) and a guilt-ridden Judas even committed suicide for betraying his innocent rabbi (Matthew 27:5). Strange things happened, too. The temple curtain demarcating the Holy of Holies was torn from top to bottom. Earthquakes shook, splitting rocks. Perhaps most alarming were sealed tombs found broken open with bodies missing, as dead saints appeared to people (Matt. 27:51–53).

Then on Sunday morning, some women went to Jesus' tomb planning to prepare his remains in compliance with Jewish burial tradition. Instead of finding his dead body, they found hope revealed–Jesus was alive!

LUKE 24:13–35

13 Now that same day two of them were going to a village called Emmaus, about seven miles from Jerusalem.

14 They were talking with each other about everything that had happened. **15** As they talked and discussed these things with each other, Jesus himself came up and walked along with them; **16** but they were kept from recognizing him. **17** He asked them, "What are you discussing together as you walk along?" They stood still, their faces downcast. **18** One of them, named Cleopas, asked him, "Are you only a visitor to Jerusalem and do not know the things that have happened there in these days?" **19** "What things?" he asked. "About Jesus of Nazareth," they replied. "He was a prophet, powerful in word and deed before God and all the people. **20** The chief priests and our rulers handed him over to be sentenced to death, and they crucified him; **21**but we had hoped that he was the one who was going to redeem Israel. And what is more, it is the third day since all this took place. **22** In addition, some of our women amazed us. They went to the tomb early this morning **23** but didn't find his body. They came and told us that they had seen a vision of angels, who said he was alive. **24** Then some of our companions went to the tomb and found it just as the women had said, but him they did not see." **25** He said to them, "How foolish you are, and how slow of heart to believe all that the prophets have spoken! **26** Did not the Christ have to suffer these things and then enter his glory?" **27** And beginning with Moses and all the Prophets, he explained to them what was said in all the Scriptures concerning himself. **28** As they approached the village to which they were going,

Jesus acted as if he were going farther. **29** But they urged him strongly, "Stay with us, for it is nearly evening; the day is almost over." So he went in to stay with them. **30** When he was at the table with them, he took bread, gave thanks, broke it and began to give it to them. **31** Then their eyes were opened and they recognized him, and he disappeared from their sight. **32** They asked each other, "Were not our hearts burning within us while he talked with us on the road and opened the Scriptures to us?" **33** They got up and returned at once to Jerusalem. There they found the Eleven and those with them, assembled together **34** and saying, "It is true! The Lord has risen and has appeared to Simon." **35** Then the two told what had happened on the way, and how Jesus was recognized by them when he broke the bread.

Filled with Questions (24:13–24)

Of the Gospel writers, Luke alone provides a detailed description of Jesus' appearance to two disciples on the road to Emmaus, a village less than 10 miles from Jerusalem.[1] Luke's account poignantly depicts the actions, attitudes, and emotions of Jesus' followers after the women returned announcing his resurrection. Why the two were headed to Emmaus is unknown, even surprising, considering the mystery surrounding the disappearance of

Jesus' body. Perhaps they were returning home after the Passover or had accommodations in Emmaus.

Their conversation focused on recent events. Probably they were piecing together the things each had seen and heard, minds whirling about what had happened or would happen. As they walked, intently analyzing motives, conversations, and events, Jesus "came up and walked along with them" (Luke 24:15). Possibly supernatural forces, divine or satanic, kept them from recognizing him, but it's also likely their state of mind limited their ability to identify Jesus. Since they weren't *expecting* Jesus to rise from the dead, they had no reason to imagine that he had joined them. Furthermore, his resurrected body, with its divine ability to appear and disappear (see John 20:19, 26) may have made him unrecognizable. Their predicament was not unusual among those to whom Jesus made post-resurrection appearances. Neither Mary Magdalene (John 20:14) nor Peter, Thomas, Nathanael, James, or John (John 21:4) recognized him; and all these were among his dearest and closest friends and followers.

Upon joining them, Jesus asked Cleopas and his companion[2] a seemingly innocuous question: "What are you discussing together?" (Luke 24:17), but it stopped the two in their tracks, surprised and visibly saddened.

Perhaps Cleopas thought this new traveling companion had been living in hole! (And he kind of had been!) Jerusalem was abuzz with all the recent events. How could he "not know the things" that happened? (24:18). Asking questions was a common pedagogical practice for rabbis, and this methodology was ultimately the means by which Jesus planned to reveal his identity to them. It's ironic and almost laughable now to consider the two disciples thought their new traveling companion was ignorant, when in fact, they were the ones who didn't know they were talking with the resurrected Jesus!

Prompted by his question, the travelers first described what Jesus of Nazareth *did*: he was a prophet (as Jesus described himself in Luke 13:32–33), and authoritative as a teacher and miracle worker "before God" (meaning *approved by God*; cf. Luke 3:22). They briefly detailed the circumstances surrounding his crucifixion. They did not hesitate to place blame on the Jewish leaders, rather than the Romans or even the multitudes, which was probably a risky thing to do, given they didn't know Jesus' identity. Next, and perhaps most importantly, the two disciples described who they'd hoped Jesus *was*: the Redeemer of Israel, the fulfillment of Old Testament (OT) prophecies such as Psalm 111:9; Isaiah 41:14; 43:14; and 44:22–24. A *redeemer* can be defined as one who *delivers, releases at a cost, or ransoms.* Unfortunately, these OT prophecies and others like them were generally interpreted as Jewish political liberation from dominating principalities. There was little to no consideration of the spiritual aspect of freeing human souls from sin. The perception of these two disciples was that with Jesus' death, the redemption they'd longed for had died with him.

Saddened as they were by the events surrounding Jesus' death, they had an even more desperate question to ponder. Women they knew and trusted had just that morning returned from visiting Jesus' tomb, announcing it was empty and claiming Jesus was alive.[3] To top it off, other friends had also gone to the tomb and found the same thing—nothing! Jesus' body was not there.

Looking for Answers (24:25–27)

On this side of the narrative, we know Jesus was alive. We know he'd fulfilled numerous messianic prophecies unrecognized by nearly every person he encountered. We know it was he who walked with Cleopas and his companion on the road to Emmaus. But for the moment, without the benefit of our hindsight or Luke's narrative, these disciples inwardly wrestled with conflicting emotions of despondency and hope.

Recognizing this inner turmoil, Jesus gently admonished the two for their inability to recognize his fulfillment of messianic prophecies. Despite their knowledge of Scripture (i.e. the Law, Prophets, and Writings), they didn't comprehend the necessary suffering of the Messiah to achieve the glory rightly due him–the glory of exaltation to God's right hand (cf. Philippians 2:5–11). Because of Scriptural misunderstandings and incorrect expectations of the Messiah–which abounded in Judaism–they interpreted Jesus' death as a failure. The Messiah's role, they believed, was to act with miraculous power, overthrowing oppressors and delivering the Israelites from all earthly enemies. This of course did not involve suffering, and the glory to be revealed should be a new and mighty king on the throne in Jerusalem. Since that had not happened, they were disappointed and assumed they would have to look for hope elsewhere.

Thus, still incognito, Jesus methodically attempted to bring enlightenment by revealing himself with biblical evidence. He interpreted the things he did and experienced with a view toward his fulfillment of each prophecy. By doing so, Jesus validated the truth of what believers today affirm as the Old Testament. He proved he did not come to abolish, but to fulfill the Law and Prophets (Matt. 5:17; cf. Romans 1:2). He understood taking time to lay a foundation of Scriptural truth would prepare their hearts and minds for him to reveal his identity.

Hope Revealed (24:28–35)

The impromptu lesson progressed as the three advanced toward Emmaus. As Cleopas and his companion neared their destination, they invited Jesus, who appeared to be traveling on, to stay with them for the night. The invitation was not terribly unusual, since hospitality, even to pagans, was considered a virtue.[4] Since the main meal of the day in Jewish custom was near sunset, the timing of their arrival was ideal for requesting Jesus' presence at their table, and he consented to their invitation.

Often, when we invite church staff members to our home for meals, we ask them to say grace. It wasn't very different in the first century. At the table that evening, since Jesus was clearly a learned teacher, the two would naturally have offered him the opportunity to give thanks and take the first serving of bread. Jesus obliged by taking the bread and offering thanks, but then, rather than taking the first serving as a guest would, he took on the role of a servant-host. He distributed the bread to others, in perfect keeping with his own character and teaching (cf. Matt. 20:26; 23:11; Mark 9:35; 10:43; Luke 22:26–27; John 13:13–16).

Suddenly, this act revealed his identity. Although these two weren't present at the Last Supper, they potentially had seen Jesus break bread at other meals or at the feeding of the multitudes. Perhaps there was something uniquely intimate about the way he gave thanks or characteristic about the way he tore the bread. Whatever it was, their "eyes were opened" (Luke 24:31), and no longer was it merely the words of Scripture revealing him as Messiah. They now "recognized" (Gr. epegnosan: "knowing decisively or certainly") without a doubt the physical revelation of the Jesus they'd known and followed. He was indeed alive! Their blindness, whether supernatural or by accident, was removed, and at that moment, Jesus disappeared from their view.[5]

For a moment, they were stunned; I imagine them looking at each other with wide eyes and slackened jaws. Then all the pieces came together, and they rushed to explain to one another that they should have realized from all Jesus taught (lit. opened or revealed to) them on the road that he was indeed the resurrected Messiah!

They didn't keep this good news to themselves! At once, they got up from the table and rushed back to Jerusalem, completely assured Jesus was alive. The contrast between their countenances and steps from Jerusalem and faces and paces returning to it, surely were as different as night and day. Upon their arrival, they found the Eleven disciples (minus Judas) also celebrating an appearance of their resurrected Lord to Simon Peter (24:34; cf. 1 Corinthians 15:5). Then they told those gathered all that transpired with Jesus as they walked to and arrived in Emmaus.

Encountering Jesus, as Cleopas and his traveling companion did, is exemplary of the numerous ways Jesus personally involved himself in the lives of others as seen in Luke's Gospel. Jesus' heart for meeting unique, individual needs challenges us as his disciples. We should live intentionally and intimately with those around us for the purpose of serving as his witnesses to all the nations (Luke 24:47–48).

Ready to Believe?

The Christian faith is not solely based on Jesus' empty tomb, but also on the testimony of those who claimed they saw him resurrected. Numerous people were martyred for declaring that truth. Jesus' physical revelation to them as recorded in Scripture and history, proves he exhibited power over death (cf. Revelation 1:18).

But, honestly, that's not enough. Taking someone else's word for it doesn't make it real in our hearts. Jesus revealed himself resurrected to more than 500 people (see 1 Cor. 15:3–8), and he desires to reveal himself to us. While he may choose physical manifestation, we need to be open to the revelation of his identity through Scripture, other believers, and even creation (see Rom. 1:20).

The Emmaus road disciples needed Jesus to reveal he was indeed their long-awaited Messiah, and that hope was truly alive. As they journeyed, he prepared their hearts with words from Scripture, so that when he broke the bread, they could believe. How do you need Jesus to reveal himself to you? As Savior? Friend? Forgiver? Healer? Deliverer? Reconciler? Provider? Perhaps a journey through Scripture is your starting place, too. Are you ready to believe?

LIVE IT OUT

Several resurrection appearances were associated with meals (see Mark 16:14; Luke 24:40–43; and Acts 1:4). Perhaps this explains why so many churches hold fellowships with food; we're inviting Jesus to reveal himself!

Consider sharing a meal with a small group, inviting each participant to share a passage of Scripture that Jesus has used in his/her life to reveal himself. If you have an imaginative group, set an empty place at the table or act out Jesus giving thanks and breaking the bread. Discuss the passages you've shared and compare/contrast your emotions and responses to those of the Emmaus disciples.

WHAT ARE YOU TALKING ABOUT?

The two disciples walking toward Emmaus were talking (Gr. *homiloun*) about and discussing (*suzetein*) with one another (*allelous*) everything that happened (Luke 24:14–15). *Allelous* can mean to *throw back and forth*, a picture of conversation tossed like a ball. *Suzetein* can be understood as debate. *Homiloun* is the word from which *homiletics (the art of preaching)* is derived, because early preaching was frequently conversational in nature (cf. Acts 8:26–40; 13:43; 18:26; 20:11; 24:26). When Jesus joined the two disciples, he used their discussion of current events as a platform from which to explain Scriptural truths.

Often the greatest evangelistic impact 21st century Christians can have is to direct our conversations toward biblical truths as we engage with people one-on-one. We can use discussions about current events like Jesus did, or informally chat with people we regularly encounter. While it's important to have a plan for leading someone to salvation or expressing your testimony, sometimes the best words we can offer are authentic dialogue. People want to have their questions heard; we don't have to know all the answers and present them as a polished sermon. Responding in love and with Scripture lets the Holy Spirit convict and work (John 16:8, 13) as he sees fit. We're not accountable for someone else's response, just our own obedience to the Great Commission.

So what are you talking about? Will you let Jesus and his word join the conversation?

QUESTIONS

1. Jesus used current events to start a conversation in order to explain Scriptural truths. What current (or personal) event can you use as a platform for sharing the hope of God's word with someone? Identify with whom and when you might have that opportunity. Pray for God's peace and favor as you prepare to share.

2. Although we often try to hide the condition of our hearts, we really do express our feelings through our countenances, particularly our eyes. Is there someone you know whose eyes reveal a hidden story of sadness or a need for hope?

3. Imagine you are Cleopas or his companion and a stranger begins to speak with you about the events of the last week. How do you describe Jesus of Nazareth? How boldly do you profess your hope in him? Do you actually blame your religious leaders outright for his execution? Do you dare mention that people you know claim to have seen him resurrected?

4. How differently does the story end if the two disciples do not invite Jesus to stay and dine with them? Do they eventually believe the other resurrection accounts or do they remain despondent and hopeless? Have you invited Jesus to engage with you? He'll come if he's invited (see Rev. 3:20).

5. Why do you think Jesus suddenly disappeared from sight when they realized it was him? Was he teaching them interaction with him would no longer be based on his physical presence? Was he revealing his divinity in a new way? Something else?

NOTES

1. Mark 16:12–13 briefly mentions it.

2. Tradition records Cleopas as Jesus' uncle, Joseph's brother. If so, even Jesus' own family members didn't recognize him following his resurrection! Theories abound regarding the identity of Cleopas' companion. Because the companion is unnamed in a patriarchal culture, it's possible the second traveler was a woman, perhaps Cleopas' wife.

3. In Jewish tradition, the spirit of the deceased hovered over the body for three days following death then left for Sheol, ending any chance for resuscitation. Thus, these disciples were convinced Jesus' resurrection was impossible.

4. Of course, among believers hospitality was expected in obedience to Jesus' teachings (Matthew 25:34–40). However, even non-believers thought hospitality was a virtue and public responsibility. If strangers were mistreated, a community's honor and religious security were risked, and pagan Greeks believed strangers were under special protection from Zeus—patron god of guests—avenging wrongs done to them or blessing those who showed hospitality. From *Living Faith in Daily Life*, "Welcoming (Even) the Stranger," BaptistWay Press, 2010, p. 65.

5. Cf. other miraculous departures in Luke 1:38; 2:15; 4:13; 9:33; Acts 1:9; 10:7; 12:10.

CHRISTMAS LESSON

Good News of Great Joy for All People

MAIN IDEA

Jesus is good news of great
joy for all people.

QUESTION TO EXPLORE

How should we respond to the
good news of Jesus' birth?

STUDY AIM

To praise God for Jesus' birth and to
share this good news with all people

QUICK READ

God revealed his glory when he
announced to the shepherds the
good news of the Messiah's arrival.

On a very typical day, I had just returned to work after a typical lunch. What I found on my desk was hardly typical. So rare was the sight, that I had never seen it before and would never see it again. Sure, the flowers that were sitting on my desk were typical of a florist delivery service. There was nothing atypical about the card attached to the flowers either. But the message they bore would change my life forever.

"Congratulations, it's a girl!"

My secretary asked if the flowers were from my wife. "If they're not, I'm in trouble!" I exclaimed. They were from my wife. And I was not in trouble. But, the good news I received that day marked me, and I would never be the same again. Good news has a way of doing that to us.

LUKE 2:8–20

8 And there were shepherds living out in the fields nearby, keeping watch over their flocks at night. 9 An angel of the Lord appeared to them, and the glory of the Lord shone around them, and they were terrified. 10 But the angel said to them, "Do not be afraid. I bring you good news of great joy that will be for all the people. 11 Today in the town of David a Savior has been born to you; he is Christ the Lord. 12 This will be a sign to you: You will find a baby wrapped in cloths and lying in a manger." 13 Suddenly a great company of the heavenly

host appeared with the angel, praising God and saying, [14] "Glory to God in the highest, and on earth peace to men on whom his favor rests." [15] When the angels had left them and gone into heaven, the shepherds said to one another, "Let's go to Bethlehem and see this thing that has happened, which the Lord has told us about." [16] So they hurried off and found Mary and Joseph, and the baby, who was lying in the manger. [17] When they had seen him, they spread the word concerning what had been told them about this child, [18] and all who heard it were amazed at what the shepherds said to them. [19] But Mary treasured up all these things and pondered them in her heart. [20] The shepherds returned, glorifying and praising God for all the things they had heard and seen, which were just as they had been told.

The Glory of Good News (2:8–12)

The night's routine was a familiar experience for the shepherds. After a day of endless weaving and meandering with the flock, it was time to settle down. The sheep had already been fed and taken to a refreshing watering hole. But the coolness of the night and the darkness that enveloped them wouldn't completely relieve the shepherds of their responsibilities. The sheep still needed to be watched.

This was the life of a shepherd. It was nothing like the life of a carpenter, who got to work in town and never had to roam the countryside chasing stray sheep. The shepherd's life was certainly not anything like the life of a scribe. Scribes had the privilege of working indoors and had the respect of the community.

Yes, shepherds were never the first to know of significant events. They weren't privy to the latest nation-changing news. No prominent delegations ever put them at the top of their visitation list. Until that night.

It would be a first for the angels, too. They were familiar with their usual surroundings—heaven, God's throne, the glory of God. They were used to being sent by God, and often with life-changing messages. That night would be no different.

Luke described the magnificent results of God's intentional interaction between the simple shepherds and the divine messengers. "An angel of the Lord appeared to them, and the glory of the Lord shone around them, and they were terrified" (Luke 2:9). Experiencing the glory of God can be a terrifying experience! The good news of the Messiah's birth was coupled with a manifestation of God's glory. The shepherds' experience that night would set a precedent for how God would continue to reflect his glory on the earth.

Through Christ, and his work in us, God would continue to reveal his glory to man. The manner in which he would do so would vary immensely from the shepherd's starry night experience. God would reveal his glory in Christ Jesus (John 8:54). He was able to use sickness "for God's glory so that God's Son may be glorified through it" (John 11:4). Someday, according to John's description, the New Jerusalem will be lit by God's glory (Revelation 21:10–11).

But what about God's glory today, after the shepherds' experience and before Christ's return? God still wants to reveal his glory on the earth. And you can be the messenger. You have been brought (Hebrews 2:10) and called into God's kingdom and glory (1 Thessalonians 2:12). As his follower, "the Spirit of glory and of God rests on you" (1 Peter 4:14). Christ has promised that "if you believe, you will see the glory of God" (John 11:40).

There are millions of people going about their regular routines. Some have shepherd-like jobs. Many are expecting nothing more than a typical day or night. All of them need to experience the glory of God. You have been called to bring a uniquely divine message to an all too common existence. Share the good news of the Messiah's birth and share the glory of God with the world.

The Shepherd's Way—Trust and Obey, Believe and Go (2:13–15)

But it would get even better. As if one angel sighting was not enough for one night, an entire company of angels appeared. The heavenly choir praised God and proclaimed his favor (Luke 2:14). Wherever the "highest heaven" might be, glory must be given to God. And for those who abide in simpler places on earth—like shepherds and us—we receive the favor of God. And that restful favor brings peace.

The glory of God was revealed, good news was delivered, companies of heavenly hosts appeared, and angelic praises rang out. And then it was over. Having experienced such a vivid display from the Lord, what was a simple shepherd to do? There was perhaps no better response from the shepherds to the message from the Good Shepherd than the response they expected from their own sheep—trust and obey.

The shepherds trusted the angel's message that today "a Savior has been born" and you will find him "wrapped in cloths and lying in a manger" (Luke 2:11–12). There was a consensus among the shepherds, "Let's go to Bethlehem and see this thing that has happened, which the Lord has told us about" (2:15b). Their trust in the message of the Messiah was so great, they were willing to leave their sheep, their families, and their homes to go to Bethlehem. First, they believed. Then they obeyed.

The Jesus the shepherds would find in the manger would grow up and reveal his glory as the Son of God. Typical men—fishermen, tax collectors, doctors, tent makers—would follow him. He would tell his disciples to "go into all the world, and preach the good news to all creation" (Mark 16:15). Like the shepherds, the disciples believed and then they obeyed.

The Jesus the disciples followed would eventually die on a cross and be raised on the third day. The glory of God would be revealed in his resurrection. He would challenge all who believed in him to become his "witnesses in Jerusalem, and in all Judea and Samaria, and to the ends of the earth" (Acts 1:8). Like the disciples, those followers believed and then they obeyed.

Now it is up to you to follow the pattern established by the shepherds, continued by the disciples, and entrusted to all believers. If you've heard the glorious good news that Jesus died for our sins and came to give us abundant life, it's time for you to believe. If you have already believed, it is time to go in obedience. What's keeping you from following in the shepherds' footsteps?

Spreading the Amazing Word (2:16–20)

The shepherds found the baby just as the angel had described, lying in the manger (Luke 2:16). Earlier, the shepherds' encounter with God's messenger resulted in obedience. Now, the shepherds' encounter with God's Messiah resulted in witnessing. "They spread the word concerning what had been told them about this child" (2:17). Their witness was a simple act—they told what they knew about the Christ child.

Today, some Christians are intimidated by the idea of *witnessing*. They imagine loud street preachers standing on a busy corner. They picture themselves having to walk down a neighborhood block and knock on an unknown door. They begin to shake at the thought of striking up a spiritual conversation with a complete stranger. But, being a witness for Christ continues to be a simple act. You simply share what you have heard, seen, or experienced with God.

Imagine yourself on a street corner (don't worry; you're not screaming a sermon through a bullhorn). Like the shepherds on that glorious night, you are not doing anything that's particularly special. Then it happens right in front of you—you hear brakes squealing and a blue car runs a red light and hits a black truck. Emergency personnel show up and a policeman asks you if you were a witness to the accident. You respond, *Officer, I can't be a witness. I am not an expert on the law. I don't know how the traffic light system works. I don't know enough math to calculate how fast the car was going or what the force was upon impact. I am not qualified to be a witness!*

The police officer asks you to take a deep breath and simply asks, *What happened?* Your answer is, *I heard brakes squealing and the blue car ran the red light and hit the black truck.* Your response fulfills your duty as a witness. You told what you heard, saw, and experienced.

It is similar in being a witness for Jesus. God is not calling you to be an expert in theology. You don't have to know the Greek and Hebrew root words of your favorite verses. He is not looking for expert debaters. He simply seeks witnesses.

Remember when you found yourself searching for something more from life and you heard God speak to you through a sermon? How about the time you were facing a difficult challenge and you were encouraged by a Bible passage or devotional? Recall the time when you sensed the presence, peace, or strength of God?

Share with others what happened when you experienced God in your life. You may be surprised by how many respond to your witness in the same way people responded to the shepherds' witness. "All who heard it were amazed at what the shepherds said to them" (Luke 2:18).

Know that the blessing of the Good News comes full circle. It all began with the angels praising God in the midst of glory revealed. Then, the shepherds bore witness and others were amazed. However, it wasn't over after they returned to their sheep. "The shepherds returned, glorifying and praising God for all the things they had heard and seen" (Luke 2:20). God will continue to be glorified and praised as we trust and obey the message of the Messiah and bear witness of what we have heard and seen!

Applying This Truth to My Life

The good news of Jesus' birth brought about a glorious experience. God chose to share this *uncommon* experience with those who some might call *common* shepherds. The shepherds believed the Messiah message and followed through in obedience. The result of their obedience was that many were amazed, and ultimately God was glorified.

Consider your response to the news that Jesus was born so that one day he would take our sins to the cross, die, and rise again to give us new and abundant life. Has this news impacted you as much as it did the shepherds? If not, do as the shepherds: trust and obey. If so, share the good news with someone today.

Savior, Christ, and Lord

We find three titles for Jesus in the angel's declaration, "today in the town of David a Savior has been born to you; he is Christ, the Lord" (Luke 2:11). Savior (sōtēr) is a term meaning deliverer or preserver. Jesus is the Savior of those who believe (1 Timothy 4:10). Through the Savior's kindness and love, he saves us, washes, and renews us, and empowers us with his Spirit (Titus 3:4–6). Those who have been delivered from sin, will receive a welcome into the Savior's kingdom (2 Peter 1:11).

Christ (Christos) means *anointed one.* God has anointed Christ as "the apostle and high priest" (Hebrews 3:1) and "heir of all things" (Hebrews 1:2). The Lamb has also been anointed "Lord of lords and King of kings" (Revelation 17:14).

Lord (kyrios) refers to someone who is a master or who is in control. The Holy Spirit empowers us to confess Jesus as Lord (1 Corinthians 12:3). Ultimately, we can only serve one lord (Matthew 6:24).

Is Jesus your Savior, Christ, and Lord?

BE A WITNESS

- Find someone who is part of your daily routine—a cashier, waitress, teacher, etc.—and think of a way to shine God's glory into their lives.

- Think of someone who would require extra effort on your part to reach (finding their contact information, driving out your way to go see them, etc.). Commit to share some good news with them this week.

- Write down something that you have witnessed God do in your life. Before the day is over, share your testimony via text, email, or post on your social network.

QUESTIONS

1. Why do you think God chose to first send the Messiah message to shepherds?

2. Do you recall a time when you saw the glory of God? What was your response?

3. Which part of God's message, revealed in the Bible, has been the hardest for you to trust?

4. Describe a time when your trust in God's word resulted in obedience?

Our Next New Study

(Available for use beginning March 2014)

JEREMIAH AND EZEKIEL:
Prophets of Judgment and Hope

JEREMIAH: SPEAKING GOD'S TRUTH UNDER PRESSURE

Lesson 1	Commissioned to Deliver God's Message	Jeremiah 1
Lesson 2	Hear God's Message	Jeremiah 7:1–16
Lesson 3	The Folly of Ignoring God	Jeremiah 18:1–12; 19:1–15
Lesson 4	When Serving God Is Hard	Jeremiah 11:18—12:6; 17:14–18; 20:7–18
Lesson 5	No Stopping God's Message	Jeremiah 36
Lesson 6	When You're Not Where You Want to Be	Jeremiah 29:1–14
Lesson 7	When God Is Unpatriotic	Jeremiah 21:1–10; 38:1–6
Lesson 8	God's Promised Restoration	Jeremiah 31:27–34; 32:1–15

How to Order More Bible Study Materials

It's easy! Just fill in the following information. For additional Bible study materials available both in print and online, see www.baptistwaypress.org, or get a complete order form of available print materials—including Spanish materials—by calling 1-866-249-1799 or e-mailing baptistway@texasbaptists.org.

Title of item	Price	Quantity	Cost
This Issue:			
The Gospel of Luke: Jesus' Personal Touch—Study Guide (BWP001167)	$3.95	_____	_____
The Gospel of Luke: Jesus' Personal Touch—Large Print Study Guide (BWP001168)	$4.25	_____	_____
The Gospel of Luke: Jesus' Personal Touch—Teaching Guide (BWP001169)	$4.95	_____	_____
Additional Issues Available:			
Growing Together in Christ—Study Guide (BWP001036)	$3.25	_____	_____
Growing Together in Christ—Teaching Guide (BWP001038)	$3.75	_____	_____
Guidance for the Seasons of Life—Study Guide (BWP001157)	$3.95	_____	_____
Guidance for the Seasons of Life—Large Print Study Guide (BWP001158)	$4.25	_____	_____
Guidance for the Seasons of Life—Teaching Guide (BWP001159)	$4.95	_____	_____
Living Generously for Jesus' Sake—Study Guide (BWP001137)	$3.95	_____	_____
Living Generously for Jesus' Sake—Large Print Study Guide (BWP001138)	$4.25	_____	_____
Living Generously for Jesus' Sake—Teaching Guide (BWP001139)	$4.95	_____	_____
Living Faith in Daily Life—Study Guide (BWP001095)	$3.55	_____	_____
Living Faith in Daily Life—Large Print Study Guide (BWP001096)	$3.95	_____	_____
Living Faith in Daily Life—Teaching Guide (BWP001097)	$4.25	_____	_____
Participating in God's Mission—Study Guide (BWP001077)	$3.55	_____	_____
Participating in God's Mission—Large Print Study Guide (BWP001078)	$3.95	_____	_____
Participating in God's Mission—Teaching Guide (BWP001079)	$3.95	_____	_____
Profiles in Character—Study Guide (BWP001112)	$3.55	_____	_____
Profiles in Character—Large Print Study Guide (BWP001113)	$4.25	_____	_____
Profiles in Character—Teaching Guide (BWP001114)	$4.95	_____	_____
Genesis: People Relating to God—Study Guide (BWP001088)	$2.35	_____	_____
Genesis: People Relating to God—Large Print Study Guide (BWP001089)	$2.75	_____	_____
Genesis: People Relating to God—Teaching Guide (BWP001090)	$2.95	_____	_____
Ezra, Haggai, Zechariah, Nehemiah, Malachi—Study Guide (BWP001071)	$3.25	_____	_____
Ezra, Haggai, Zechariah, Nehemiah, Malachi—Large Print Study Guide (BWP001072)	$3.55	_____	_____
Ezra, Haggai, Zechariah, Nehemiah, Malachi—Teaching Guide (BWP001073)	$3.75	_____	_____
Psalms: Songs from the Heart of Faith—Study Guide (BWP001152)	$3.95	_____	_____
Psalms: Songs from the Heart of Faith—Large Print Study Guide (BWP001153)	$4.25	_____	_____
Psalms: Songs from the Heart of Faith—Teaching Guide (BWP001154)	$4.95	_____	_____
Amos. Hosea, Isaiah, Micah: Calling for Justice, Mercy, and Faithfulness—Study Guide (BWP001132)	$3.95	_____	_____
Amos. Hosea, Isaiah, Micah: Calling for Justice, Mercy, and Faithfulness—Large Print Study Guide (BWP001133)	$4.25	_____	_____
Amos. Hosea, Isaiah, Micah: Calling for Justice, Mercy, and Faithfulness—Teaching Guide (BWP001134)	$4.95	_____	_____
The Gospel of Matthew: A Primer for Discipleship—Study Guide (BWP001127)	$3.95	_____	_____
The Gospel of Matthew: A Primer for Discipleship—Large Print Study Guide (BWP001128)	$4.25	_____	_____
The Gospel of Matthew: A Primer for Discipleship—Teaching Guide (BWP001129)	$4.95	_____	_____
The Gospel of Mark: People Responding to Jesus—Study Guide (BWP001147)	$3.95	_____	_____
The Gospel of Mark: People Responding to Jesus—Large Print Study Guide (BWP001148)	$4.25	_____	_____
The Gospel of Mark: People Responding to Jesus—Teaching Guide (BWP001149)	$4.95	_____	_____
The Gospel of John: Light Overcoming Darkness, Part One—Study Guide (BWP001104)	$3.55	_____	_____
The Gospel of John: Light Overcoming Darkness, Part One—Large Print Study Guide (BWP001105)	$3.95	_____	_____
The Gospel of John: Light Overcoming Darkness, Part One—Teaching Guide (BWP001106)	$4.50	_____	_____
The Gospel of John: Light Overcoming Darkness, Part Two—Study Guide (BWP001109)	$3.55	_____	_____
The Gospel of John: Light Overcoming Darkness, Part Two—Large Print Study Guide (BWP001110)	$3.95	_____	_____
The Gospel of John: Light Overcoming Darkness, Part Two—Teaching Guide (BWP001111)	$4.50	_____	_____
The Book of Acts: Time to Act on Acts 1:8—Study Guide (BWP001142)	$3.95	_____	_____
The Book of Acts: Time to Act on Acts 1:8—Large Print Study Guide (BWP001143)	$4.25	_____	_____
The Book of Acts: Time to Act on Acts 1:8—Teaching Guide (BWP001144)	$4.95	_____	_____
The Corinthian Letters—Study Guide (BWP001121)	$3.55	_____	_____
The Corinthian Letters—Large Print Study Guide (BWP001122)	$4.25	_____	_____
The Corinthian Letters—Teaching Guide (BWP001123)	$4.95	_____	_____

Hebrews and the Letters of Peter—Study Guide (BWP001162)	$3.95	_____ _____
Hebrews and the Letters of Peter—Large Print Study Guide (BWP001163)	$4.25	_____ _____
Hebrews and the Letters of Peter—Teaching Guide (BWP001164)	$4.95	_____ _____
Galatians and 1&2 Thessalonians—Study Guide (BWP001080)	$3.55	_____ _____
Galatians and 1&2 Thessalonians—Large Print Study Guide (BWP001081)	$3.95	_____ _____
Galatians and 1&2 Thessalonians—Teaching Guide (BWP001082)	$3.95	_____ _____
Letters of James and John—Study Guide (BWP001101)	$3.55	_____ _____
Letters of James and John—Large Print Study Guide (BWP001102)	$3.95	_____ _____
Letters of James and John—Teaching Guide (BWP001103)	$4.25	_____ _____

Coming for use beginning March 2014

Jeremiah and Ezekiel: Prophets of Judgment and Hope—Study Guide (BWP001172)	$3.95	_____ _____
Jeremiah and Ezekiel: Prophets of Judgment and Hope—Large Print Study Guide (BWP001173)	$4.25	_____ _____
Jeremiah and Ezekiel: Prophets of Judgment and Hope—Teaching Guide (BWP001174)	$4.95	_____ _____

Standard (UPS/Mail) Shipping Charges*			
Order Value	Shipping charge**	Order Value	Shipping charge**
$.01—$9.99	$6.50	$160.00—$199.99	$24.00
$10.00—$19.99	$8.50	$200.00—$249.99	$28.00
$20.00—$39.99	$9.50	$250.00—$299.99	$30.00
$40.00—$59.99	$10.50	$300.00—$349.99	$34.00
$60.00—$79.99	$11.50	$350.00—$399.99	$42.00
$80.00—$99.99	$12.50	$400.00—$499.99	$50.00
$100.00—$129.99	$15.00	$500.00—$599.99	$60.00
$130.00—$159.99	$20.00	$600.00—$799.99	$72.00**

Cost of items (Order value) _____

Shipping charges (see chart)* _____

TOTAL _____

*Please call 1-866-249-1799 if the exact amount is needed prior to ordering.

**For order values $800.00 and above, please call 1-866-249-1799 or check www.baptistwaypress.org

Please allow three weeks for standard delivery. For express shipping service: Call 1-866-249-1799 for information on additional charges.

YOUR NAME   PHONE

YOUR CHURCH   DATE ORDERED

SHIPPING ADDRESS

CITY   STATE   ZIP CODE

E-MAIL

MAIL this form with your check for the total amount to
BAPTISTWAY PRESS, Baptist General Convention of Texas,
333 North Washington, Dallas, TX 75246-1798
(Make checks to "BaptistWay Press")

OR, **CALL** your order toll-free: 1-866-249-1799
(M-Fri 8:30 a.m.-5:00 p.m. central time).

OR, **E-MAIL** your order to our internet e-mail address:
baptistway@texasbaptists.org.

OR, **ORDER ONLINE** at www.baptistwaypress.org.

We look forward to receiving your order! Thank you!